A Woman
to Blame
The Kerry Babies Case

NELL MCCAFFERTY

Attic

First published in 1985 by Attic Press
Attic Press is an imprint of Cork University Press,
Youngline Industrial Estate
Pouladuff Road, Togher
Cork, Ireland
Reprinted with a new Foreward 2010

British Library Cataloguing in Publication Data

McCafferty, Nell
    A woman to blame: the Kerry Babies case.
    1. Hayes, Joanne—Trials, litigation, etc.
    I. Title
    364.1'523'0924 HV6541.172K4
ISBN–13: 9781855942134

Printed by ColourBooks Ltd, Baldoyle, Co. Dublin
Typeset by Tower Books, Ballincollig, Co. Cork

www.corkuniversitypress.com

Attic Press wishes to thank the publisher Faber and Faber for permission to
reproduce an extract from Seamus Heaney's collection *Door into the Dark*
(1969), p. 22.

The publishers gratefully acknowledge permission from the following to
reproduce photographs: John Carlos/*Sunday Tribune*, Ray Cullen/*Irish Press*,
The Irish Times, Pat Keegan/*Irish Press*, Gerry Kennelly/*The Kerryman*, Ronan
Quinlan/*Irish Press*, Derek Speirs/*Report*, *Sunday Tribune*, *Magill*.

It will not escape the notice of the reader that all the photographs reproduced
in this book are by men. Attic Press went in search of the best photographs
available and we found the best. For those aware of our publishing policy to
promote women in all areas of our work you will also be aware of how disap-
pointing and problematic it was for us to be unable to locate, after much effort, photographs by women. It was felt the book would be unfinished without
photographs and a decision was therefore taken to go ahead.

Dedicated to

Cathy Harkin, Derry, 1939–1985

Contents

Main Characters

FAMILY AND FRIENDS

Joanne Hayes

Kathleen Hayes
Joanne's sister

Ned Hayes; Mike Hayes
Joanne's brothers

Mary Hayes
Joanne's mother

Bridie Fuller; Joan Fuller; Sister Aquinas
Joanne's aunts

Mary Shanahan
Hayes family cousin and neighbour

Mary O'Riordan; Martina Rohan
Joanne's work colleagues and friends

Jeremiah Locke
Father of Joanne's children

GUARDS

Superintendent John Courtney;
Detective Sergeant Gerry O'Carroll;
Detective Sergeant P.J. Browne
From murder squad in Dublin

Detective Dillon; Detective O'Donnell
Detective Smith; Detective Coote
*Kerry police involved in interrogation of
Hayes family on 1 May*

Guard Liam Moloney
*Local Abbeydorney policeman, friendly
with Hayes family*

LAWYERS

Justice Kevin Lynch
Tribunal judge

Michael Moriarty

James Duggan
Counsel for judge

Kevin O'Higgins
Counsel for Attorney General

Anthony Kennedy
Counsel for guards

Martin Kennedy

Dermot McCarthy
Counsel for Hayes family

Brian Curtin

Patrick Mann
Solicitor for Hayes family

DOCTORS

John Harbison
State pathologist

Declan Gilsenan
Deputy state pathologist

John Creedon
*Gynaecologist (treated Joanne after the birth
in St Catherine's hospital)*

Liam Hayes
Hayes family doctor

Aidan Daly
*Liam Hayes's partner (referred Joanne
to hospital after birth)*

John Fennelly
*Chief psychiatrist at Limerick psychiatric hospital
(treated Joanne after arrest)*

Robert McEneaney
Physician (examined Bridie Fuller)

Francis Chute
GP *(did not examine Bridie Fuller)*

Robert Harrison
Obstetrician (called as expert witness)

Brian McCaffrey
Psychiatrist (called as expert witness)

Calendar of
Events

25 June 1982	Mary Locke's first child is born
19 May 1983	Joanne's daughter Yvonne born
23 December 1983	Relationship between Joanne Hayes and Jeremiah Locke ends
6 April 1984	Joanne's regraded job advertised
13 April	Joanne's son is born and dies
14 April	Body of baby boy found at Cahirciveen
25 April	Mary Locke's second child is born
1 May	Hayes family taken in for questioning by police
	Joanne charged and taken into custody
2 May	Body of Joanne's baby found on farm at Abbeydorney
11 May	Joanne released from Limerick psychiatric hospital, where she had been transferred from Limerick prison
10 October	Charges against Joanne dropped
Mid-October	Internal police inquiry set up, which proves inconclusive
28 December	Tribunal of inquiry, set up in response to public outcry, meets for first time
14 June 1985	Tribunal meets for last time

Prologue

In the opening days of the 'Kerry babies' tribunal a married man went to bed in a Tralee hotel with a woman who was not his wife. He was one of the forty-three male officials – judge, fifteen lawyers, three police superintendents and twenty-four policemen – engaged in a public probe of the private life of Joanne Hayes.

When this particular married man was privately confronted with his own behaviour, he at first denied it. Then he crumpled into tears and asked not to be exposed. He had so much to lose, he said. 'My wife . . . my job . . . my reputation . . .' He was assured of discretion.

No such discretion was assured to Joanne Hayes, as a succession of professional men, including this married man, came forward to strip her character. The lawyers, doctors and police were guaranteed the full protection and licence of law to do so. The priests who had dealt with her were not called to testify and the Catholic Church stayed silent through the whole affair. However, the Church has ways of making itself heard: when it was all over, the priests of her parish refused to say Mass in her home.

This is the story of professional men, the lawyers, doctors, police and priests, who found woman to blame. It is also the story of one woman and the 'Kerry babies' tribunal.

Introduction

It was medieval. A group of men put a young unmarried woman on the stand and questioned her about the exact circumstances of the conception and birth and death of her newborn baby. She came from a tiny village in the west of Ireland. They had come down from the capital, Dublin. The Pope had just come and gone from Ireland. The men wondered aloud if the woman had in fact given birth to two newborn babies who had been found dead in Kerry, though blood tests showed that she could only have been mother to one. The men put forward and examined for six months a theory of superfecundation, which postulates that a woman can conceive of twins by two men if she has sexual intercourse with both in the space of twenty-four hours. 'There were times when we all thought she had twins,' said the presiding judge, Justice Kevin Lynch.

The legal men and a succession of male doctors, psychiatrists and police officers – forty-three in all – spent six months probing the young woman's mind and body. A doctor gave the dimensions of her vagina during a previous birth. Ordnance Survey maps were used to pinpoint the exact locations of the places where she had sexual congress with her married lover. The question was asked, 'Did she love this man or what he and other men were prepared to do with her?'

It was medieval, but it happened in 1985. The probing of the woman's sexual history brought the men gathered round her to such a fever pitch that she collapsed. She was excused, temporarily, and could be heard retching and sobbing in the corridor. The judge ordered that she be sedated and then brought back to testify. She gave evidence in a daze, her head bobbing off the microphone. The judge asked that her friends keep a suicide watch on her that night.

The country was sickened, and showed support for Joanne Hayes by sending her flowers and Mass cards. When the inquisition finally ended, the country rapidly changed, by constitutional vote, and a new Ireland came into being. It was forged on the anvil of Joanne Hayes' suffering. Never again, the changes showed, would one woman be held to blame for the ills that had beset Ireland. Or, at least, never again would an exclusively male panel sit in judgment of one woman.

To understand what was done to Joanne Hayes, and why, and how much has changed as a result of that, it is necessary to set a context. When John Paul II came to Ireland in 1979, he preached against contraception, divorce and women's work outside the home. There had been stirrings of modernity on the island, thanks to the Irishwomen's Liberation Movement, founded in 1970, and accession to the European Union in 1972. The IWLM demand for the legalisation of contraception had met with popular support, and opposition from state and Church. The sale or advertisement of contraceptives was illegal and punishable by penal servitude. The legal prohibition on married women engaging in paid work outside the home had been lifted in exchange for massive European funding, though the enforced entry of women into the paid workforce was treated with reluctance by business, trade unions and parliament. At the time of the ending of the marriage bar in 1975, less than ten per cent of married women were in the workforce, and single women were mostly confined to work in the unskilled service sector.

Still, the appetite among women for freedom from the kitchen sink was growing. There had been growing unease at state-sanctioned punishment of those women who had incurred state or Church displeasure. The punishment had been aimed mainly at single mothers, whose children were deemed illegitimate in law, an official sanction of bastardy that the Catholic Church relished. It was normal to incarcerate single mothers in Magdalene homes run by the religious, usually until their children were adopted, but often for life. Thousands of Irishwomen, in succeeding generations since the foundation of the state, had thus been spirited away and forced to put their children up for adoption. Others escaped to England and came home childless. This seems medieval now. It was normal right up to the legal crucifixion of Joanne Hayes, who had defied sanction by giving birth to and rearing her first child at home, and holding down a paid job.

It seems ridiculous now that divorce was unobtainable in Ireland until 1996, though marital breakdown and separation had been steadily increasing. Even more puzzling, on the face of it, is that the IWLM did not include a demand for divorce among the six demands published in its initial manifesto. It is not that we lacked courage. It is, simply, that the demand did not occur to us in Catholic Ireland, the Constitution of which expressed state approval of the special position of the Catholic Church. We had little or no idea how a woman who was forbidden the right to work might survive, usually with children, after marital breakdown. At that time the children's allowance was paid to the father. There was no welfare payment for separated wives. Women in financial need relied on the discretionary judgement of a Poor Law officer. There was no knowledge, much less recognition, even among us, of the extent of wife-battering in the home. There were no refuges for such women. There was grim stoic acceptance of the adage that if you make your bed, you must lie in it. Romance and sex had little to do with marriage, within which, as the late Nuala Fennell put it, women faced a nightmare of unremitting pregnancy. Six children per marriage was the norm, often exceeded.

Though our plight was ostensibly sad, all our feminist wars were merry. In the heyday of the Seventies, the laws against

Irishwomen were so self-evidently silly that taking aim at them was like shooting fish in a barrel. Then the Pope came. The Irish lived easily with the contradiction of adoring him while simultaneously breaking his edicts. So did some priests – an effective underground network made known which clerics would give absolution for what were, officially, mortal sins. It was in the aftermath of the papal visit that civil hell was visited upon Catholic Ireland in the form of a constitutional referendum on abortion.

Scarcely had John Paul departed these shores than a tiny group of right-wing, ultra-conservative Catholic lay people, mostly medical practitioners, visited parliament to announce that abortion could and would be introduced into Ireland via a loophole in the Constitution. In the space of two hours, these people wrung astonishing commitments from a Fianna Fáil government and the main opposition Fine Gael that the constitutional loophole would be closed. The fight to save fertilised eggs was on. The country was put through a crash course on such hitherto unknown facts as the existence of zygotes. In the space of two years, three governments came and went. Bishop Joseph Cassidy declared with smug certainty that the most dangerous place in the world was in a woman's womb. The Constitution was amended in November 1983 to give the fertilised egg a right to life that was equal to that of the woman in whose body it was growing. The era of the unborn was upon us.

Joanne Hayes conceived during that time of perfervid dictat. Her baby died after it. The men were sent to find out what had happened to the fertilised egg they had spent years theoretically defending. After they had filleted her to their satisfaction, the judge pronounced that 'she had hit her newborn baby with a bath brush, after giving birth, to make sure that it was dead.' One cannot, of course, kill a dead baby, but damage to Hayes was done by the judicial implication that she wanted the child dead.

A measure of his temperament and attitudes to women in the Kerry babies case is the judicial pronouncement made at its end by Justice Lynch. He asked, 'What have I got to do with the women of Ireland in general? What have the women of Ireland got to do with this case?' He presumed to lecture Irish women on what he saw as their misguided support for Hayes in her agony, by sending her flowers and Mass cards. He found that the 'most wronged woman' in the matter was Mary Locke, the wife of Jeremiah Locke who had fathered Joanne's babies. 'Why no flowers for Mrs Locke?' he asked. 'Why no cards or Mass cards? Why no public assemblies to support her in her embarrassment and agony? Is it because she married Jeremiah Locke and thus got in the way of the foolish hopes and ambitions of Joanne Hayes?'

Mary Locke's reply to his query was simple, dignified and devastating for Lynch. She declared, 'Joanne Hayes was harshly treated.'

After the waters closed over this vile and cruel episode in Irish life, the spotlight swivelled onto Irish holy men. It was discovered in 1992 that a Catholic bishop, Eamon Casey, had fathered a child by a young woman who had been placed in his care; that he had tried to force adoption upon her; that she had been sent back to America whence she came; and that he had rifled Church funds to contribute to his secret son's upkeep. The child was conceived in 1974. The bishop had shortly afterwards sold a Church-owned hospital to a private medical consortium on condition that no sterilisations were performed in it, a condition to which the medical men happily subscribed.

During his affair, the bishop of Kerry had availed of the clerical network which allowed him to confess his sexual sins every morning and receive absolution before saying daily Mass. The bishop had welcomed the Pope to a youth Mass in Galway in 1979, then set off in defence of the unknown fertilised egg.

The rapid decline of the Catholic Church is dated from the revelation of his philandering. Unlike its incarceration of unmarried mothers, the Church found a posting for Casey in South America, and brought him back to Ireland when it adjudged that the fuss had died down. He still retains his title.

The decline was hastened by the further revelation that the bishop's sidekick on the altar from which the Pope was serenaded by the duo, the priest Michael Cleary, had fathered two children by his housekeeper, who had come to him in distress as a teenager in 1967, and who lived with him in the priest's house until his death in 1993. Cleary had been a particularly vulgar and crude leader of the pro-life brigade. He announced on his national radio show that wearing a condom was akin to wearing socks in the bath. Known as one of the 'singing priests' cabaret show, he would joke onstage that 'you can kiss a nun once, you can kiss a nun twice, but you mustn't get into the habit.'

He, who denied the existence of his own children, infamously brought severely disabled children (cherished by their mothers) onto television to promote his case against abortion.

National tragedy turned to farce when it was revealed that Cleary, father of two, had confided his actions in Casey, father of one, and that Casey had admonished him to mend his ways.

Church reaction to Cleary's common-law wife and son was to evict them from the parish house.

Farce turned to horror when it was revealed that a paedophile priest had been knowingly sheltered by the Church, and given further access to children. The holy men considered the protection of their institution more important than the protection of children.

Horror turned to despair when it became known that the Church had given sanctuary and protection to thousands of holy men who had systematically sexually abused thousands of children since the foundation of the state. The abuse was perpetrated especially on orphans, bastards and the children of the poor who had been sent by the state into Church care in institutions – though hospital chaplains were found to have abused sick and crippled children and the practice of child sex abuse by parish priests was also widespread.

Despair turned to disbelief when it was revealed that the Vatican knew of such abuse, worldwide, and kept secret files on the abuse. The woman who first revealed the nature of this abuse, Christine Buckley, was vindicated by the publication in 2009 of the Ryan Report into clerical abuse. Buckley's insistence that the somewhat sanitised report be fleshed out with intimate detail of what exactly had been done to children was magnificent. Thanks to her, it would be impossible henceforth to bury the sexual sadism of clerics under a blur of bland statistics. Ms Buckley, a fount of righteous anger, told the nation on television and radio and in print exactly how bureaucrats went about deciding what compensation should be paid to the victims of holy men: 'They sat there and asked adult plaintiffs to estimate how much of the penis was inserted into the anus, when they were children.' Television history was made when the former mayor of Clonmel, Michael O'Brien, spoke at length of how some Rosminians held him down and raped and beat him. Catholic Ireland was dead and gone and its adherents numbed.

Revelations of what had been done by holy men who crusaded in support of equal human rights for the unknown fertilised egg were followed by a ghastly confirmation of where such a fetish would lead. The legalisation of abortion, in severely restricted circumstances, was introduced in 1992 after the X case erupted. A fourteen-year-old girl, raped and impregnated by an acquaintance, was brought to England by her parents to secure an abortion. The parents asked Irish police if DNA from the aborted foetus might be used to secure a conviction against the rapist. The state moved instantly to obtain a court order, which demanded that the parents return to Ireland, with the pregnant child, or face charges and possible imprisonment if they procured an abortion for her outside the jurisdiction. Frightened, they brought their pregnant suicidal daughter home to face her doom.

In face of absolute citizen outrage against internment of the child in Ireland, the Supreme Court convened and found that abortion could be allowed when the life of the mother is threatened by suicide.

Threats to a mother's health, as opposed to her life, are still not considered grounds for abortion. This cruelty to pregnant women obtains even where it is medically certain that a diseased foetus will not live seconds beyond birth.

In the wake of the X case and in exchange for a multi-million injection of funds from the EU, the people voted to allow freedom of travel abroad for an abortion, and freedom of information about abortion at home. That EU funding is generally acknowledged to have given birth to the Celtic Tiger era. The fate of eggs,which are fertilised in Ireland and then exported troubles the Irish not at all. As ever, uncomfortable problems are exported to England and a blind Irish eye is turned to them. The men of medicine disgraced themselves again in the course of yet another referendum to refine and impose further limitations on the original amendment on fertilised eggs. The three masters of Dublin's maternity hospitals gave a press conference to announce their intention to throw their weight behind it. Under questioning from a now less subservient media, they admitted that their real preference was that termination should be allowed in cases where a damaged foetus would not long survive birth. The proposed amendment failed. The Dáil has yet to act to bring legislation into line with the expressed national vote that abortion be permitted in limited circumstances.

The situation of Irishwomen is not, however, bleak. Where contraception is concerned, the change is startling. Where once any reference to contraceptive practice was banned, television now carries happily and casually brazen narrative ads from the state-funded Crisis Pregnancy Agency. For instance, a young woman is seen going upstairs and into the bedroom with a young man. Her mother calls the daughter. 'Have you taken your pill?'

In another ad, a heterosexual couple are kissing heavily in a fish-and-chip shop. The waitress, delivering their order, asks, 'Would yeez like a condom with that?' Condoms are displayed for sale in supermarkets, pubs and pharmacies, in varied flavours and sizes and strengths.

Fine Gael minister Nuala Fennell abolished the bastardisation of children in the aftermath of the Kerry babies case, and homosexuality was decriminalised by Fianna Fáil minister Máire Geoghegan-Quinn. Senator Mary Robinson, political adviser to the IWLM, was elected president of Ireland in 1992 and served two successive terms, as did her successor Mary McAleese. Though women otherwise failed to make a breakthrough in parliamentary representation, and are fewer in number now than they were before the Kerry babies case, Irishwomen have broken new ground in formerly barren places. Married or single, they now make up nearly half the workforce. The Magdalene houses are closed, and orphan-placement agencies at an effective end. Crèches for the children of working parents flourish, in a society where double-income families are now the norm. The birth rate has shrunk to less than three children per family, and advances have been made with regard to equal pay and equal opportunity, which is now a trade union mantra.

As against that, marital breakdown has increased and divorce is common. Divorce is not a sign of success in human relations, but it does herald an adult willingness to deal honestly and openly and legally with human failure. Abortion rates are high, albeit conducted elsewhere. Again, the rates do not signal success but a mature acceptance that conception and birth does not always guarantee a happy or desired outcome. The fact that contraceptive practice is not yet the norm among sexually active teenagers signals that sex education still leaves much to be desired.

Women now do two jobs – working outside the home by day, and rearing a family by night, albeit men do a little more housework than they used to, and can be seen interacting with their children.

The recent calamitous collapse of the Celtic Tiger has seen the government attempt to push women back to the kitchen sink. Besides losing jobs, women have suffered the double cut of reduction in the family allowances which helped them pay for the childcare that allowed them to take up paid work. The funding of women's groups around the country has been savagely reduced and the worst cut of all was applied to the Employment Equality Agency, a frontline defender of the rights of women workers. Its budget was halved, an action which rendered it virtually toothless and forced the head of the agency to resign in protest.

However, in sum, Irish people are in a much better state than they were at the time of the Kerry babies case, if one takes sexual health as the norm against which we are to measure ourselves – and it seems an eminently reasonable measurement. To meet, mate and make a nest, with or without babies, is precious – there are many forms of living together, in community, and these forms do not always include a partner in the home, or sexual congress. Friendship is precious. Joanne Hayes and her family were sustained in their ordeal by the friendship of neighbours and, especially, women friends.

The writings of Annie Proulx are illuminating about the nature of love and sexuality. In one of her short stories, 'Them Old Cowboy Songs', she writes of a damaged cowboy. He cried when his woman gave him little love bites. He cried because nobody had ever loved him like that. 'I ain't never been. Loved. I just can't hardly stand it' – and he began to blubber 'feel like I been shot', pulling her into his arms . . .

Before the Kerry babies, we were all, in one way or another, damaged cowboys – taking unloving bites out of each other, usually in the name of self-proclaimed holy men, who effectively abolished God and imposed their wretched man-made rules upon our behaviour, aided and abetted by the men of law and medicine and the Dáil. Virginia Woolf had it right when she wrote 'There it is, then, before our eyes, the procession of the sons of educated men, ascending those pulpits, mounting those steps, passing in and out of those doors, preaching, teaching, administering justice, practising medicine, making money.'

And inflicting damage untold on we who are cowboys.

Those days of barbarism are effectively over, though much remains to be done. A single startling example will suffice. It would be considered barbaric nowadays for a couple, hetero-sexual or gay, to walk down a wedding aisle as virgins; to commit themselves legally to a lifelong relationship, civil or religious, without first living together; to delude themselves that a certificate of marriage means certainty.

It is very much the norm nowadays, before making such a commitment, to first live together, and then make a baby. The old order of marriage, home and baby has been completely reversed to home, baby and commitment.

The nightmare that was an Irish honeymoon has vanished. It used to be that a couple brought a towel on honeymoon to absorb the blood that would allegedly flow after the woman had been penetrated by a battering ram known as the penis. Today, most sexually active people happily and enthusiastically engage in sexual congress, equipped with contraception. Horrific exceptions apart – and they are many – the day of the damaged cowboy is done, as is the day of the damaging cleric, doctor, lawyer and elected politician.

We are not fully healthy yet, but we are getting there and it is wonderful.

1. The Cahirciveen
Baby

The tombstones in the graveyard of Cahirciveen, County Kerry, seldom record when a person was born. They boast, rather, of the longevity achieved by those now dead: 'Margaret O'Sullivan, aged 95', says one; John Keating was ninety when he finally passed on. The cemetery bears proud testimony to one advantage of existence in a small quiet town on the western Atlantic seaboard, in Ireland's most scenic county – people live a long time. 'There are two kingdoms, the Kingdom of God and the Kingdom of Kerry' goes the local saying.

Cornelius O'Sullivan, whose body was brought back from New York in 1982, died in his prime, you might say, worn out by the rigours of life in a big city. He was only seventy-seven. Had he remained on Valentia, the island in the bay overlooked by the cemetery, he might have lived until he was ninety-six, like E.J. Ring, whose tombstone gives the recipe for a vigorous, fulfilled life in the twentieth century: 'A GAA [Gaelic Athletic Association] man all his life, a fenian forever.'

The tombstones of these women and men, aged ninety-six, ninety-five, ninety, eighty-four, eighty-one, eighty, eighty-nine, eighty-four, range like affronted sentinels around an anonymous grave marked by a plastic mock-marble cross, on which a local undertaker has spelt out a message in printer's transfer lettering: 'In loving memory of me, the Kerry Baby.'

The words are gently reproachful. The 'me' demands a response. Who am I? Where did I come from? I belong to Kerry. I was the Kerry baby. All that is known about this boy-child is that he was born and died within the space of

1

forty-eight hours leading up to 8.30 pm on Saturday 14 April 1984. After birth, his umbilical cord was cut flush with his belly, he was washed, his neck was broken and he was stabbed twenty-eight times in the neck and chest.

He was found dead, face down, wedged in the rocks on the White Strand beach, three miles from Cahirciveen. A local farmer found him. Jack Griffin had jogged along the small, narrow, sandy crescent and, just before he turned up on to the grassy field that grew right down to the shore's edge to check on his cows, he spotted the infant. He thought it was a doll. On his way back across the beach he looked again and found the naked baby. It was not the first time that human or animal remains had been found on the sand. The large plastic fertiliser bags that litter the shore testify to the farming of the fields that surround it. For instance, just before lawyers made their final submissions on what came to be known as the Kerry babies case, an evening stroll on White Strand showed four such bags, torn and holed and filled with sand, and the half-covered corpse of a dog.

The bags and the dog might have come from the fields or been washed up by the sea. A woman who regularly used the beach, as do all the people of Cahirciveen in summer, once found a frogman's flipper there, with sock attached. She brought it home for the amusement of her children. When they had washed out the seaweed that clogged it they found bones inside. The guards (police) traced the flipper and sock to a man on Valentia Island, which stops up the mouth of the bay, who had hired out the diving suit seven years before. The diver had subsequently been lost, presumed drowned, off Beginish Island, which lies between Valentia and White Strand.

Now, seven years later, his foot had washed ashore. It had taken all that time to travel a couple of hundred yards. The guards notified the man's parents, who had long ago accepted his death. They left the disposal of the bones to the police.

The guards, following established practice, gave the foot a Catholic burial in Cahirciveen cemetery. The limb is held to be an essential part of the whole, and, where the trunk of a body is missing, the limb serves as the symbolic remains.

This theological problem of what exactly constitutes a human body, and a human being, had convulsed Kerry and Ireland in the year 1982–83, when the country had considered amending its Constitution to ensure that abortion would be outlawed for all time. The Catholic Church announced that life began at conception and threw its weight behind what came to be known as the pro-life amendment campaign.

There was much learned discussion conducted by priests, lawyers and doctors as to whether or not a fertilised egg was a human being. The Catholic Church said that it was. So, too, in a signed statement did seventy-four of the ninety doctors, obstetricians, gynaecologists and radiologists then working in the Kingdom of Kerry.

The debate, in gruesome detail, had gripped the attention of the nation. Many of the details were to be repeated in the public inquiry that followed the finding of the Kerry baby. Those details were to be flashed around the world. Ironically, it was on the shore of White Strand at Cahirciveen that the first transatlantic telegraph cable linking the old world with the new was laid in 1850.

The burial of the Cahirciveen baby was an emotional occasion. Local schoolchildren provided an escort from the undertaker's to the cemetery. Some of them had seen the infant in its coffin. Previously, during the anti-abortion campaign, some of these children had been shown film slides of a preserved foetus in a jar. 'The most dangerous place to be at the moment is in the mother's womb' they had heard Bishop Joseph Cassidy say on national radio just before the campaign votes were cast. Now, a mere seven months later, they escorted to its grave a baby that had safely escaped the womb, only to meet instant death.

The death of babies, in or out of the womb, was no stranger to them. Between the successful passage of the amendment in September 1983 and the discovery of the Kerry baby in April 1984 the schoolchildren of Cahirciveen had held a day-long seminar, under the supervision of their teachers, on the life and death of one of their peer group, Anne Lovett. On 30 January 1984, the fifteen-year-old schoolgirl had been found dying in a grotto devoted to the Virgin Mary, in Granard, County Longford. Alongside her lay the corpse of her new-born son. The young mother perished of childbirth and exposure. Three weeks later, her fourteen-year-old sister apparently killed herself. Nobody knew why these things had happened. It was officially regarded as a private family tragedy. The Cahirciveen schoolchildren told their teachers that their parents were the last people they would turn to for help if they found themselves pregnant. Families could not cope with that sort of thing, they said.

2. Babies Everywhere

After the state's only pathologist, Dr John Harbison, had pronounced the Kerry baby murdered, the guards began to search for its parents. The local police chief, Superintendent Donal Sullivan, began his investigation in the most conversational way, talking to people he met in Cahirciveen on the Sunday night of his return from Killarney, where the post-mortem had been held.

He confirmed later, to a lawyer for the tribunal, that the purpose was 'to get the rumour around and get the word on the streets'. That way there was a better chance of getting information, he said. He also circulated a questionnaire to each family, which the police collected when it was filled in. The schoolchildren were all individually questioned.

Cahirciveen has a population of 1,428. The collated information profiled an Irish town, where such features are not normally given public recognition. Families were named where incest was suspected; a married man was having an affair with a young woman; the female partners in broken romances were checked out; women who had to get married because of pregnancy were reported; a woman was nominated whose husband had been barred from her home on foot of a court order.

The search spread beyond the town. Hippies were reported and investigated. Travelling families got visits from the police. A man with a criminal record and a common-law wife was checked out. The police visited a man who merely had 'a female living with him' and was in a different category entirely, as was the married woman who had 'a man' living with her. Information was given on a pregnant woman known to have paid a visit to England. A ten-year-old girl said her next-door neighbour was 'after having a baby'. The police were even given the name of a woman who had been pre-scribed certain tablets to help in her pregnancy. The name of the informant was confidential, of course.

Confidence was not always preserved, however. An elderly man who had been imprisoned during the IRA campaign in the Fifties, and gone on hunger strike in pursuit of political status, did not take kindly to the garda (police) visit. He thought himself, mistakenly, the object of what he perceived to be renewed state harassment. The police reassured him that they only wanted to talk to him in connection with what he might have seen on his evening walks on White Strand. 'So and so' had mentioned that this was his custom. Later, the elderly man visited 'so and so' and grumbled that the ancient Irish political custom of never telling the police anything had been betrayed.

One woman did benefit from the unexpected intrusion into her private life. The baby to which she had secretly given birth in her family home four months before, causing her to with-draw totally from the public gaze and stay indoors, was officially registered after a visit from the guards, and she was persuaded by a welfare officer to apply for the unmarried mother's benefit of fifty-one pounds a week. Now she walks the streets openly with her child. She and her mother, with the child in the pram, are still to be seen daily scavenging the town dump. A financial safety net of some kind has been provided.

The net which the police threw over Cahirciveen, and neighbouring Waterville and Killorglin and Sneem and Glencarr, around the tourist trail of the Ring of Kerry in fact, yielded nothing. The woman whom a nurse had seen walking on the road by White Strand was innocent. The father of a fifteen-year-old girl had noticed that she mentioned rape in her diary, but nothing came of this, though the police established that her parents were 'responsible'.

The gravedigger had kept a watch on the Kerry baby's grave and no mother had returned to it. The priests had appealed from the pulpits in vain. A light plane seen flying over the area before the baby's death had been checked out and no parcel had been thrown from it.

Have you noticed anything unusual, anything at all, the guards asked whoever they met. There were twenty-eight guards looking everywhere. One of those guards was to go home, later, and be awakened in the night by his wife to be told that their daughter had gone unexpectedly into labour in the bedroom next door. The baby was subsequently adopted.

3. Suspect Family

In the second week of the woman-hunt some members of the crack Dublin murder squad had come down to help. They were Kerrymen by birth. Their leader was Superintendent John Courtney, who was reared in the north Kerry mountain village of Anascaul. Detective Sergeants Gerry O'Carroll and P.J. Browne hailed from Listowel, a market town on the plains which hosted an annual writers' week, under the benign eye of local playwright and short-story writer John B. Keane, whose literary excoriations of the tortured rural sexual psyche were renowned. Gerry O'Carroll was wont, in the course of the tribunal, to quote verbatim from Germaine Greer's *Sex and Destiny*. He referred listeners particularly to her chapters on coitus interruptus and infanticide. P.J. Browne was the writer of police reports.

As the local guards swept south Kerry, Detective Sergeant Dillon, stationed in the county capital, Tralee, in north Kerry, was asked to make his own enquiries in that town. He made three phone calls.

The first was to CURA, the Catholic organisation that helps unmarried mothers. CURA had been established in Kerry in October 1983 in the wake of the anti-abortion campaign. In contrast to the seventy marriage counsellors which the Church provided for the Kingdom, CURA had only three. The existence of these three counsellors was not widely known. After the Cahirciveen baby was found, they had sent an anonymous letter to the county paper, *The Kerryman*, advising women who needed their help to make contact with them by ringing their head office in Limerick or Cork.

CURA counsellors have to remain anonymous because they also function as social workers, in the employ of government, and there is a conflict of interest. The police, of course, know exactly who the counsellors are.

Detective Dillon's friend in CURA could not help.

He then made an equally fruitless call to his contact in the Bon Secours hospital. His contact in St Catherine's hospital, however, gave him precise and detailed information of three unmarried women who had been in the maternity ward, in or around the time the Cahirciveen baby had been discovered. Detective Dillon's contact furnished alibis for two of the three women, declaring that CURA 'was looking after them and was fairly satisfied with both positions'.

The hospital, nominally controlled by the state, is run by the Sisters of Mercy nuns, who work closely with CURA.

There was an 'inconclusive file' on the third woman, Joanne Hayes, said the contact. She had come into the maternity ward on 14 April a few hours before the Cahirciveen baby was found. The file on her read 'scan and uterus recently emptied'.

It had taken the detective exactly ninety minutes to come up with her name. Hours later he went out to the hospital and spoke to John Creedon, the gynaecologist who had treated her.

Mr Creedon was one of those doctors who had signed a public statement declaring that the unborn child needed protection. His superior, Mr Doyle, also signed the 'pro-life' statement, because he was willing to supply married women with an intra-uterine contraceptive device. It was known locally that these doctors had uncomplimentary rhyming nicknames related to their distaste for artificial methods of birth control.

Joanne Hayes had told him that she had not had a baby, Mr Creedon told Detective Dillon, though the compelling evidence of the scan, which he had twice taken of her womb, suggested otherwise. He was keeping an open mind.

Mr Creedon was used to women coming into hospital for treatment after secret home births. In eight years he had attended five of them. He said that eventually they would all admit to a dead baby somewhere, and would be persuaded to bring the body in for a coroner's report. There was never any need to involve the police. In this instance, he had determined that eventually he might have to consult his solicitors. 'If we are in doubt, what is our position?' Ultimately the question should be addressed to the ethical committee of the medical register council, said the man who had appealed to voters with such assurance during the 'pro-life' campaign.

Joanne Hayes stayed in his hospital for six days, and was then released by him to make her own way in the world. During her stay, he stressed, he had asked the hospital chaplain, Father Quinlan, to speak with her. The chaplain, who is also head of CURA in Kerry, is of course bound by confidentiality in both roles. He can only report back to Mr Creedon if the patient authorises him to do so. Father Quinlan did not report back. The hospital notes showed, though, said Mr Creedon, that after speaking with the priest his patient was 'recovered somewhat in spirit though depressed in demeanour'. He sometimes referred distressed patients to a psychiatrist, said Mr Creedon, but in this case had not done so.

His patient had now been referred to the police. He knew that they were looking for the mother of the Cahirciveen baby. He advised them that they were on the wrong track. If they should go and look around Abbeydorney, he placed the matter in their hands, they would probably find her baby there. He did not consider Joanne Hayes to be the kind of demented woman who would have stabbed her baby to death. She had the same demeanour as all those other women who had come sadly into hospital with voided wombs and a missing infant. She also had, as Detective Dillon knew by now, the perfect profile of a prime suspect in the case. Before he went to see Mr Creedon, he had gone out to Abbeydorney to speak to the village's only policeman, Liam Moloney.

Guard Moloney had known that Joanne Hayes was pregnant, but had not connected that pregnancy with the Cahirciveen baby. In fact, he had written 'No suspects' in the questionnaire sent to all police stations some days previously. There was one sure way of checking, said Guard Moloney, and he rang Joanne's cousin, Mary Shanahan.

Mary Shanahan told him Joanne had miscarried in hospital. Guard Moloney told Detective Dillon what Mary Shanahan had just told him. Detective Dillon told Guard Moloney what the hospital had said. There was a query about the miscarriage. Guard Moloney then told Detective Dillon about the Hayes family.

There are less than two hundred families in Abbeydorney and Guard Moloney, who had been stationed there for seven years, knew the people well. He knew the Hayes family, who lived two miles outside the village on the way to Tralee, particularly well. Their sixty-acre scrub farm had passed on to the family through the lately deceased Maurice Fuller, sole brother of Joanne's mother Mary. Maurice Fuller had been a peace commissioner, and the guards used to go up to the house regularly to have things signed by him. The farm effectively supported two families. In the ancestral family dwelling, a long single-storey house, Maurice Fuller had lived with his spinster sister Bridie, a nurse. A hundred yards away, in a small county-council cottage, lived his sister Mary, her husband Paddy Hayes and their children Kathleen, Ned, Mike and the youngest, Joanne.

The brothers-in-law Maurice Fuller and Paddy Hayes worked the farm, milking sixteen cows and rearing a similar number of cattle for beef. Bridie Fuller, the unmarried sister, worked in St Catherine's hospital, the four Hayes children went to school and Mary Hayes kept both houses. She established her domestic headquarters in the old farmhouse, and everyone ate there by day and mingled there by night.

The Hayes family had never adapted to the confined quarters of the little council house and its location on the main road. For two years after it was built, they used it as a place to store grain and farm materials and continued to live in the Fuller home. The farmhouse was thatched with straw, and water had to be fetched from the well, but it was home to Mary Hayes, and the council dwelling with its modern conveniences was not. Eventually they had to move there for sleeping purposes to comply with the contract of tenancy, but real life was firmly centred on the farmhouse. It had been that way for as long as she could remember.

II

Mary Fuller's father, a primary-school teacher, had married into the farm and Mary was eventually chosen to help keep domestic order in what had become an extended family. As well as her father's elderly in-laws, the unmarried brother and sister of his wife, there were Mary's own brothers and sisters, Maurice, Kitty, Bridie and Joan.

Maurice was chosen to run the farm and the others moved out into the world. Kitty trained as a teacher and went off to a convent, where she became Sister Aquinas. Bridie trained as a nurse, joined the British army and was sent off to Malaya. Joan went off to London to take up domestic service.

Mary never left the homestead. In all her life she had never held a paid job. Sometimes she cleaned the home of an elderly neighbour, and was given a few shillings.

Abbeydorney during Mary's teenage years is vividly recalled by Tom Shanahan, now a retired police inspector. In 1935, he says, there was widespread depression caused by Éamon de Valera's economic war with England, of which Ireland was still a colony. Dev had refused to hand over land annuities and the British responded with an embargo on all Irish agricultural produce. This became known as the tariff war. 'The birth of a calf became the saddest event on Irish farms. Within twenty-four hours of its birth the calf was slaughtered and its skin sold to obtain a bounty of ten shillings offered by the government for the skin of a new-born calf.'

Secondary education was a privilege. Those who could afford it cycled long distances to the nearest town. In Abbeydorney parish there were four motor cars, three of them used for hackney work. The bicycle, the ass and cart, the pony and trap were the modes of transport. Radios were few and far between. There was no electricity. The paraffin-oil lamp and the candle illuminated the darkness. Street lighting outside of cities was non-existent, and the beckoning light of distant countries was dimmed. The worldwide depression brought emigration to the USA to a standstill and few could get work in England.

In 1935 two significant events occurred. The Catholic Young Men's Society (CYMS) was formed in Tralee and thousands attended the inaugural meeting. The priest who addressed them underlined the evil of industrial action, which caused strikes and a drop in productivity, urged the abolition of trade unions and 'class warfare', recommended respect for employers, stated that the Russian Revolution of 1917 had brought economic chaos in its wake, warned against red infiltration in Ireland, advanced the poverty of his audience as proof that it had already occurred, and asked them to join with him in the fight against communism. He was cheered to the rafters and the young men formed a branch of the CYMS called 'Our Lady of the Assumption', in memory of the direct ascent from earth to Heaven of a woman without sin who did not suffer the pangs of punishing death.

Then there was a move against dancing. The parish dance halls that afforded entertainment 'were regarded by the clergy of the time as a threat to the morals of the youth', and a Public

Dance Halls Act was passed in February 1935 to regulate their control. The priests came to court when applications for a licence to run the halls were being heard and some succeeded in having their own conditions written into the licence. One of the most bizarre was the condition known as the three-mile limit. This meant that if a man or a woman lived more than three miles from a dance hall, he or she could not legally enter that hall. The intent of this was to preserve the morals of the local community. The gardaí were under clerical pressure to enforce this limit and a number of prosecutions were brought.

Confined at home, crowded onto farms with no prospect of work outside them, or cherishing the notion in unsettled foreign places that one day they'd come back and make a proper home, the rural people of the time were distinguished in one notable respect: either they did not marry or they married late.

Mary Fuller was the only one of her family to marry. She married the man who grew up beside her, one field away, when she was thirty-four years of age. It was then 1954 and Paddy Hayes came to live in the farmhouse with her and her aunt and Maurice Fuller and Bridie Fuller, who had returned from Malaya to nurse her dying mother and never gone away again. Paddy Hayes helped Maurice Fuller run the farm, Bridie had a job in Tralee hospital and Mary kept house. The next generation came along.

III

Four children were born of the marriage – Kathleen in 1954, Ned in 1957, Mike in 1958 and Joanne in 1959 – and Mary Hayes reared them from her lifelong vantage point, the range in the kitchen in the farmhouse in which she had been born. To her countrywoman's eye, the council house that was built in 1963 was fit only for sleeping in.

After the deaths of her husband in 1975 and her brother Maurice in 1976, the farm was run by Mary's son Mike. Kathleen had an office job in a laundry in Tralee, Ned was making van deliveries for a wine merchant and Joanne was just about to go to commercial college. Aunt Bridie was in premature retirement, due to illness.

As the Eighties opened, this was a relatively stable and peaceful country family, established locally for generations, well respected, with active roots in the community.

Kathleen was a member of Macra na Feirme, the young farmers' organisation, and a member of CARE, a voluntary organisation that looked after the elderly and arranged annual outings for them. Maureen Moloney, wife of the local guard, was also in CARE. Kathleen babysat for her and her husband. Kathleen was a dedicated follower of the local hurling and football teams, travelling all over the county to watch them play. There was a friendly rivalry between her and Guard Moloney, who was a native of Cork city. When the Kerry and Cork teams should meet, Kathleen would shout 'Up Kerry' and Liam would shout 'Up Cork'.

Ned was even more passionate. He was secretary of the Abbeydorney branch of the GAA. Besides the football and hurling, he had personally set up a ladies' football team. His pursuits patterned those of Uncle Maurice, after whom the local football pitch, Fuller Park, had been named, and like his late uncle he joined the Abbeydorney drama group. Ned would cram as many footballers as he could into Aunt Bridie's car, drive the team to a match and finish off his evenings with a pint in the village, in the Silver Dollar pub. This was his world; he was a sociable fellow and he was content.

Mike did not have a world beyond the farm. He had gone once to Killarney, twenty-five miles away, and once to Listowel, twelve miles away. Mike's world was cows. Mike would talk about cows until the cows came home and had long gone to sleep. You would go to sleep yourself talking to

Mike about cows, for he was slow of speech and of thought, and his brow would furrow with the effort of making up words and sentences. He was inclined to shy away with a physical start, like a nervous young animal, if any topic other than cows was introduced, but when he'd realise that the stranger's intentions were friendly his brown eyes would clear, like the sky breaking through the clouds that constantly overhang Kerry, and he would give a delighted smile and try to reply. Eventually cows would be mentioned again, and then peace would come over him and finally conversation itself would lapse into a companionable silence, or you'd feel free to speak with whoever else was around and Mike wouldn't mind at all. He'd go back into his own world. He produced third-class milk and he was very sweet to be around.

Joanne's world centred increasingly on Tralee, where she'd secured a job as receptionist in the sports complex. She'd work the shift until six or ten in the evening and then go for a drink with her new-found friends. Saturday nights always found her back in town, at a disco or in a pub.

The family only ever had one bit of bother really, and that was discreetly handled. Ned mentioned to Guard Liam Moloney that Aunt Bridie had taken to driving while drinking. The family car belonged to her, though Ned and Mike were insured to drive it, and Ned didn't feel he had the authority to stop the owner and eldest living member of the clan from doing as she wished. Liam Moloney handled the matter with supreme tact. He rang Sister Aquinas, who was teaching infants at the convent school in Ballybunion, twenty miles away. Sister Aquinas sat down and wrote a letter to her younger sister Bridie. Bridie gave up driving the car.

Aquinas was a regular visitor to the farm. She'd often stay overnight. Sometimes, though not often, because she was a nun and elderly now, she'd go with them all up into the bog to cut and foot the turf. They'd bring sandwiches and tea and work and talk in the sunshine. Joanne would join them on those summer days. For all its cosmopolitan delights, the one thing Tralee couldn't offer you was a day up in the bog, and there were few pleasures in the world like it.

Aunt Joan, the acerbic red-haired cosmopolitan of the family, had returned from London in 1969 in the year of Bridie's controversial retirement from hospital. She had stayed on the farm, with the family, doing temporary jobs in Tralee hotels and then she got a job as a priest's housekeeper in Newbridge, County Kildare, away over in the east near Dublin. She spent all her free time coming home to the farm. She'd come down at Easter, at Christmas, on the anniversary of her brother's death every 20 June and for three weeks' annual leave every September.

When Aunts Joan and Aquinas couldn't come home, they'd maintain contact every Friday by ringing Joanne at her workplace or receiving a call from her. She'd fill them in on family and local news. The calls would be short, perfunctory and friendly.

In 1982 a couple of minor disasters and the makings of a major one struck the homestead. Kathleen was made redundant. Ned was made redundant. There was Mike's small creamery cheque coming in during the summer months, Bridie's pension and Mary Hayes's widow's pension, but Joanne was the only wage-earner in the family, bringing home eighty-eight pounds a week. This family was now relatively poor, living on dole and pension and a single woman's wage. So were many other families. The recession was widespread.

Late one evening in the month of May, Kathleen heard shouting coming from the main road and then a knock came to the farmhouse door. Kathleen opened it to find a group of agitated women standing there. They wanted to speak to her mother.

Kathleen roused her mother, who was sleeping by the range, and they listened at their front door to the three women, who were all related to a man called Jeremiah Locke, who worked as a groundsman in the sports complex with Joanne. Neither Kathleen nor her mother had ever heard of him. The three angry women who faced them were Jeremiah's mother, wife and sister-in-law. His wife Mary was eight months pregnant. The sister-in-law did the talking. Joanne was having an affair with Jeremiah and they wanted the affair stopped. Of course they knew what they were talking about! The three women had, only minutes before, down on the main road, pulled Joanne out of Jeremiah's car. Joanne had walked away and Jeremiah had followed her. God knows where they were now.

Joanne did not return home that night. Jeremiah did not return to his home. They stayed with friends in a suburb of Tralee. Joanne told Jeremiah that she was two months pregnant.

The following day Jeremiah Locke returned home and was reconciled with his wife. Joanne Hayes went back out to Abbeydorney to face her affronted family. There were tears, recriminations and promises of amendment. She would see this married man no more.

Mary Locke had a baby on 25 June. Joanne Hayes miscarried on 30 June. Her relationship with Jeremiah Locke resumed in August. Her family had taken what steps they could to prevent her seeing him. There was a problem, they realised, as he used to bring her home from work of an evening. Joanne's shift work and the infrequent bus service to and from Abbeydorney did not coincide, even if the bus could have been afforded. She had relied on Jeremiah, or neighbours who used the sports complex, or hitch-hiking, or Ned on occasion. Ned used to ring her at the end of every day's shift and if she had a lift, fine, if not, he would drive in to fetch her.

Now that they were fully apprised of the situation Ned was delegated to ring Joanne daily and daily to fetch her home. This family did its best. There were days, though, when Joanne assured them that a lift had been arranged. On one of those days, towards the end of that summer of 1982, she became pregnant again by Jeremiah.

The misery of her watching family was tersely summed up by Aunt Bridie during the following Easter 1983. She met Aunt Aquinas, home for a visit, at the front door and said 'Joanne's pregnant. He's a married man.'

There was little else to be said. Joanne was happy, her family was not.

When the baby, Yvonne, was brought back in May from St Catherine's hospital, the others were slightly embarrassed. They didn't know what to say to the neighbours who called in. There was no conventional way to end the halting introduction of the child: 'This is Joanne's daughter Yvonne . . .' and the unfinished sentence would trail off into the unspeakable distance.

The neighbours quickly took up the slack, concentrating speedily, with ohs and aaahs of delight, on the infant and the mother, and never a sentence was uttered in that house about the father. Gradually Yvonne became their collective heart's delight. It had been twenty-two years since a baby's cry had been heard on the farm and the sound was as lovely as it was regenerative. She was the new generation and she belonged to all of them.

Jeremiah Locke did not belong and his continued association with Joanne was a source of heartfelt trouble to all but her. The troubled family turned, as it had helplessly turned when Aunt Bridie's drinking troubled them, to Guard Liam Moloney. Mary Hayes went down to the station and spoke with him. 'I always thought the guards were there to help you,' she said.

The young guard did help. He assured Mary Hayes that Joanne would never know who had put him on to her and, indeed, this was Joanne's first question to him when he drove up to the house one night and asked her to come outside and sit in the car with him and have a chat. He had put on a civilian jacket over his police trousers to indicate his friendly intent.

Who had asked him to talk with her about Jeremiah Locke, Joanne wanted to know. No one, he said. Who had told him?

No one in particular, he said, but it was a well-known fact that she was having an affair with a married man, that this had been a cause of disturbance on the public highway some time ago, that he wanted no trouble on his highways and that he wished to discuss this with her as a friend. There was no future for Joanne in that set-up, he said. Jeremiah Locke had a wife and a child.

Joanne told him three things in short order: that Jeremiah was unhappy with his wife Mary; that he would one day set up a home with Joanne, who was passionately in love with him; and that the whole thing was none of Guard Moloney's business.

The meeting between them took place in August, three months after the birth of Yvonne. Joanne became pregnant again by Jeremiah in or shortly after that month, though the exact date was difficult to determine, since she menstruated only once every three months. In any case she was fairly pregnant at the Christmas office party when she learned that Mary Locke was also fairly pregnant again.

Her relationship with Jeremiah Locke effectively ended that night. In their twenty-two-month relationship she had become pregnant by him three times. Joanne Hayes faced into 1984 severely burdened in mind and body. Her heart was broken, she was expecting a baby and, in February of the new year, she learned that her job was about to end.

In the early hours of Friday morning, 13 April, she gave birth in secret and hid the body of her child on the farm. All that the neighbours and Liam Moloney knew was that she had been pregnant, had been taken into hospital, and was pregnant no more. Some assumed that the baby had been adopted; some assumed that there had been no baby, but a miscarriage.

A cousin by marriage of the Hayes family, Mary Shanahan, certainly thought that Joanne had miscarried. Kathleen had been down to visit her on the night of Wednesday 11 April and had miserably confided that Joanne was pregnant 'again'.

Mary Shanahan said that she knew that. Sure most people knew that, though it wasn't their place to mention it until the family should, officially. They watched *Hill Street Blues* on television and then Kathleen went glumly home. Forty-eight hours later, on the night of Friday 13 April, she arrived down at Mary Shanahan's again to say that Joanne was bleeding heavily. 'Christ, she's had the baby,' said Mary Shanahan, and she and Kathleen and the friend who had been visiting Mary, a nurse called Elsie Moore, got into Elsie's car and drove the short distance to the farm.

They did not go inside, for fear of upsetting Mary Hayes. Kathleen fetched Joanne out to the car and watched the women drive back to Mary Shanahan's house. The doctor was telephoned. The message they gave him was necessarily garbled. In the car Joanne had said that her last period was in November, which would make her six months pregnant, but no one was sure.

The doctor was sure of one thing. If the pregnancy had been at an advanced stage and now was no more, he said, he would have to inform the police. This was his response to an emergency telephone call about a woman who was haemorrhaging. Dr Aidan Daly was one of the seventy-four Kerry doctors who had signed the anti-abortion statement.

When Joanne heard, on the way in to his surgery, that Dr Daly had mentioned the police, she was frightened. She also needed help, so she overcame her fright and went in to see him. He palpated her stomach, felt her uterus, diagnosed a threatened miscarriage, wrote out a letter, sealed it, told Joanne to hand it in at the hospital and recommended that she go there at once. Joanne did not go to hospital.

She went home that night to her family.

The following day she went into hospital. Sister Aquinas saw her before she left the house that Saturday morning. The nun had come to see how Mary Hayes was recovering from the flu that had confined her to bed for several weeks. 'I did not notice anything particularly amiss. I was very anxious and very tense myself. I found my sister Mary very sick. I found Joanne getting ready to go to hospital, possibly to stay. My sister Bridie was not well and, I think, needing a bit of care and there was a child, eleven months old, to be minded. I was wondering how Kathleen could cope with it.'

After Ned drove Joanne away, she was told how Joanne had been bleeding, with a heavy period, since the night she had gone out into the field. 'They told me she went out and she stayed out for a long time . . . no, I did not consider that mysterious.'

Next day, Sunday, Aquinas rang her friend Sister Mechtilde, assistant matron at the hospital. 'I told her that Joanne would probably be getting blood transfusions and I wanted to know would I go to the medical floor or the consultancy floor to see her and Sister Mechtilde said that Joanne was in the maternity ward . . . it was dreadful.' Sister Mechtilde brought her that evening to the maternity ward. 'I saw Joanne was in a corner lying down and it was a public ward. There were three or four other young mothers there. I sat beside Joanne's bed and I asked her how she was.'

Their sparse painful conversation was confined to the number of 'units of blood' that Joanne had received, and the 'scan' that would be done on the morrow. The implication was beyond doubt. The imagination did not need to transform words into flesh. The nun left the matter delicately there.

Subsequently, said Sister Aquinas, 'The scan showed that whatever . . . that there was nothing in the womb.' She recalled Sister Mechtilde's words exactly. 'Her words to me were that whatever was there, there was nothing there now and that is what I took from that, that there had been a miscarriage.' Joanne did not correct her impression.

IV

Joanne lost the baby in hospital, Mary Shanahan now told Guard Moloney over the phone. Guard Moloney put the phone down and told Detective Dillon, who had been standing beside him in the Abbeydorney police station. Detective Dillon told Guard Moloney that Joanne had not lost a baby in hospital and had not necessarily had a miscarriage. Guard Moloney then told Detective Dillon and Mossy O'Donnell what he knew about Joanne Hayes. Her profile as a suspect was classic.

The detectives went to gynaecologist John Creedon that night, spoke with him again over the weekend, and on Sunday night the head of the murder squad, John Courtney, came down from Dublin. Next day the entire investigation switched from Cahirciveen to Tralee. On that Monday morning, 30 April, Joanne Hayes woke to her twenty-fifty birthday and went back to work. She met Jeremiah Locke on her way into reception, sat in the car with him briefly, congratulated him on the baby that had been born to him and his wife on 25 April and said that she herself had had a miscarriage. She worked and went home.

That night John Courtney outlined to his assembled team what he wanted them to do next day with the unsuspecting Hayes family.

4. The Guards

John Courtney felt that Joanne Hayes was a woman of 'loose morals'. At his first conference he therefore advised the guards to find out if she had any boyfriends other than Jeremiah Locke. He also advised them to approach this woman with care. 'Women's minds are very peculiar at that stage, before or after giving birth,' was his opinion. He had dealt with one woman who had murdered her husband on the eve of child-birth, had been hysterical, and then was utterly calm four days later in hospital with the child in her arms.

There was another reason for caution: 'In all my years I've never yet seen a person tell the full truth about a murder.' As well as that, he had experience of people confessing to murders they hadn't committed, and he was able, from his experience, to discount their confessions, though the avail-able evidence incriminated them. There had been, for example, the case of a child in Cork, eleven years old, raped and murdered, and, though there were six points of forensic evidence to tie a certain suspect in with the crime, 'quite a good case' in fact, he ruled the suspect out. Correctly. He had investigated thirty-six people over that one, including a couple who confessed, falsely, before he charged the thirty-sixth person.

Rape, murder, political crime and kidnapping had come within his ambit as a professional policeman of thirty-seven years' standing before he got involved in the Kerry babies case. As for seeing it all, this detective had seen things people would never know about. He had personally supervised the Malcolm

MacArthur case, which had introduced a new word, 'Gubu', into the language.

Gubu is an acronym for 'grotesque, unbelievable, bizarre and unprecedented', which is how the Taoiseach (prime minister) of the time, Charlie Haughey, described the discovery of a murderer who had been given shelter in the flat of the murderer's unsuspecting friend, the Attorney General. Superintendent Courtney never did tell anyone about the look on the Attorney General's face. He just moved on to the next job and returned faithfully to the place where he was born every time his holidays came around.

He grew up in the Irish-speaking Kerry village of Anascaul in the depressed Thirties. A child of that time described it vividly in the local newspaper, *The Kerryman*. Occasionally they would come late to school, because, as was explained to the teacher, 'We had to go to the railway station to see someone off.' To America. It was like saying goodbye to someone sentenced to 'ten years' hard labour abroad'. At the station 'We all wept and were speechless with sorrow and sadness.'

For teenage boys, though, in the Forties, there was occasional light relief, especially in nearby Killorglin, to which the entire countryside repaired after the harvest for three days and nights of merrymaking, which a priest of the time described as 'the orgy of Puck Fair'. In Killorglin, then as now, a he-goat was hoisted thirty feet up in the air onto a platform, was clothed in purple and crowned king. The people fell to celebrating his coronation with feasting and drinking. The animal looked down upon this and the clergy despaired.

John Courtney left it all behind in 1948, when he joined the guards and went to live in the big cities of Cork and Dublin. Always, though, he would spend his holidays in Anascaul, working on his brother's farm, and he eventually built himself a holiday home there. Now he was home again, working on a case involving a mother and baby, father possibly unknown. He had always had problems linking men to cases involving women of the type he considered Joanne Hayes to be. For instance, 'the violent death of a girl with loose morals is one of the most difficult to investigate, because no man will come forward and say they had an association with them. If there was a man who had an association with Joanne Hayes,' apart from Jeremiah Locke, who had been positively identi- fied, 'it would be almost impossible to locate him.'

Detective Sergeant Gerry O'Carroll, a long-time colleague of Superintendent Courtney, had his own jaundiced view on paternity. Far from finding it difficult to locate the father of some other woman's child, he knew that many a man had reason to doubt the paternity of his own children. 'We live in a promiscuous society. There have been umpteen cases of neighbours getting pregnant by their next-door neighbour.'

He would not wish to cast a slur on the neighbours of Joanne Hayes, but 'all I am saying is that casual sex takes place; it doesn't have to be an affair; it doesn't have to last all night; it doesn't have to last an hour.' In Ireland today there was a promiscuous society, though of course that had always been so; it was just that, maybe, 'everything is more out in the open now'.

Eighteen years as a policeman in the city had shown him this. Also people had told him things. And he was a reader of 'letters in some of our Sunday papers in agony columns'. He was firm in his views. 'It is happening, has happened, and con- tinues to happen.' Besides which, he had Germaine Greer's *Sex and Destiny* under his arm.

To this wide range of experience and learning, Gerry O'Carroll also brought knowledge of his native Kerry, and keen eyesight. 'I have this curious idea that native Dublin women look hugely pregnant always, while I have noticed that a lot of countrywomen just don't look pregnant at all.'

An Irishman could scarce afford to blink his eyes then, lest his women have sexual intercourse with the fellow next door, and it would take a sharp-eyed fellow indeed to notice that she was pregnant, never mind know if she was pregnant by him.

Detective Sergeant P.J. Browne, fourteen years in the force, who was to interrogate Joanne Hayes next day in partnership with Gerry O'Carroll, also had a sexual philosophy. Joanne, he said, was 'the willing concubine of Jeremiah Locke'. A concubine, in his opinion, was 'a person lying down with another'.

Sergeant Browne had come down to Tralee with Superintendent Courtney the previous night and been appraised en route of the situation. He was about to deal with what he described as 'a sad tale. It occurred because a young girl in her mid-twenties was scorned by the married man she loved, had children for and wanted for herself. Hell hath no fury like a woman scorned.'

Looking back, he described the whole thing as 'grotesque, unbelievable, bizarre and unprecedented'.

Joanne Hayes and her family were about to come into sustained, intense, individual contact with these men, behind closed doors.

5. The Moral
Policemen

Long before she met these men, Joanne Hayes's life had been controlled, as the lives of all Irishwomen had been controlled, almost exclusively by men. The preserves of Church and state were predominantly male. The country's Constitution spelt out the hope that women would always know their place: 'The State shall endeavour to ensure that no woman shall be obliged by economic necessity to engage in labour outside the home.'

In 1970 a movement for the liberation of women was launched. Its primary task was to ensure that women could control their own fertility and the Constitution became the Trojan horse of their fight for freedom.

At that time contraception was totally prohibited in Ireland. The promotion, advertisement, distribution and sale of contraceptives was illegal and punishable at law. Mary McGee, a woman whose life was threatened by further pregnancies, went to court in 1976 and won the constitutional right to use birth-control devices.

If she could find them.

They were still not legally on sale in the country. A handful of voluntary family-planning clinics, located in the big cities, walked a legal tightrope by making them available in exchange for 'donations'. Charlie Haughey moved to put some semblance of order on this farce in 1979, when, as Fianna Fáil minister for health, he introduced a Family Planning Act which provided for the sale and distribution of contraceptive devices to married couples only. Advertisement and promotion of them was still banned. A conscience clause which he inserted into his Act ensured that doctors and pharmacists would fulfil the role of moral policemen: if the consciences of these mainly male, mainly Catholic practitioners forbade them to prescribe or fill prescriptions for contraceptives, married supplicants would have to go elsewhere. The doctors in turn patrolled the pharmacists, who could not sell even non-medical devices such as the condom without a prescription.

These men rose with relish to the challenge of patrolling women's wombs, accepted the Act without demur and brought their consciences to bear, with venom, upon them. There was widespread refusal to prescribe or fill a prescription, and many of those doctors who could bring themselves to accede to a married woman's plea placed further obstacles in her way by refusing to signal the elasticity of his conscience in advance. She had to interpret an elaborate code.

The Kingdom of Kerry provided an outstanding example of these moral policemen. In the county capital, Tralee, where the women's group still finds it impossible to confirm how many of the town's eight doctors approve of contraceptive practice, a young doctor has hung two posters on his waiting-room wall. One of these advertises the Billings method of natural birth control for married couples, the other gives the name and address of a faraway unmarried mother's home, where the single woman may give birth in secrecy to a child which the state officially deems illegitimate.

This doctor, waiting behind closed doors in his surgery beyond, hopes that the women who read his posters will infer that he is not averse to the idea of them seeking to determine, within marriage, the number and spacing of their children. If they should further infer that he might see his way to allow them to do so by use of artificial means of contraception, and ask him outright about this in his surgery, he will grant their request. He never, he says, initiates the conversation. However, he will not prescribe the intra-uterine device, which he holds to be an abortifacient.

Guess again, missus, and we'll see what we can do for you.

The Family Planning Act conscience clause which allows the every whim of these men to hold sway does not dictate obeisance to Catholicism. One village doctor in Kerry boasts that he will prescribe the pill, irrespective of age or marital status, to 'mentally defective women' and even to married women who 'have children annually by irresponsible husbands', though not to women impregnated annually if, in his opinion, the husbands are responsible.

The woman who successfully negotiates with such a Kerry doctor must then find a Kerry pharmacist. Most will handle prescriptions for the pill. The explanation given by one of them is illuminating. The pill, he said, has always been acceptable in law and Christian theology as a cycle regulator, and it is not for him to presume that the woman seeking it is motivated by any desire other than that of regulating her menstrual flow.

Ten of the twelve pharmacies in Tralee refuse to stock condoms, as do five of the six in Listowel, five of the six in Killarney and the sole chemist in Cahirciveen.

The consciences of even these men are patrolled by another set of moral policemen. Customs officials in neighbouring County Cork, who monitor the air approaches to the west, impounded forty-eight condoms which a Protestant Kerry doctor tried to import by post from England for his own personal use. The official letter notifying him of seizure of his contraband stated that such articles in such quantity must be imported personally and a satisfactory verbal explanation supplied as to their intended use, to safeguard against illegal sale. The doctor's wife became pregnant during the dispute.

The ultimate moral policing of the Kingdom of Kerry was conducted by the Roman Catholic Church, under its then bishop, Kevin McNamara, whose sermons were often carried verbatim in the county's biggest local newspaper, *The Kerryman*. His exhortations to his flock were as simple as they were austere. The use of artificial methods of contraception were sinful, and married couples for whom the natural methods were unsuitable should, he said, refrain from sexual relations. 'Sexual activity outside marriage is a serious sin', he proclaimed in his lenten pastoral in 1983. 'It is necessary to call things once again by their true names – fornication, adultery, lustful desires, immoral displays in cinemas, videos and etcetera.' He called for 'reverence for parental authority, self-denial and discipline for the young' and stressed the 'essential role of the wife and mother in the home'.

He had a restrictive view of her role. 'Is she prudent and economic in the management of her home? Is she loving and supportive of her husband as she ought to be? Does she do her best, according to her resources, to provide wholesome and appetising meals? Does she give enough time to her children, or to the contrary, does she absent herself from the home to a degree that is unnecessary and harmful?'

He exhorted fathers and husbands to drink much less. That was all he asked of them, that they drink much less.

To the young unmarried he recommended 'Chastity; avoid the sins of impurity; be present to another human being in a friendly, open and generous spirit, sharing thoughts and feelings with joy and gratitude and full respect for the dignity of oneself and others, as members of Christ's Body and Temples of the Holy Spirit.'

Father Joseph Nolan of Kilflynn, who normally delivers the sermon at Sunday Mass in neighbouring Abbeydorney, had a further recommendation for those unmarried young who failed to observe the Church's strictures on chastity. The use of contraception by them, he said in a television interview, compounded the seriousness of the sin because it indicated full knowledge and intention to sin before the sin was committed.

It was a brave and confident and informed woman, and one who was willing moreover to disregard the teachings of her Church, who could beat her way through this thicket to the safe haven where the protection of birth control was available.

A Tralee woman in her twenties with third-level education in another part of the country behind her went, after graduation, to her local doctor to renew her prescription for the pill. She was, he knew, due to marry her long-standing fiancé. He refused to fill out the prescription. She had to take the train to Dublin, to a doctor of her acquaintance, to avoid further humiliation.

She then had to attend a pre-marriage course, to qualify for a Catholic Church ceremony in Tralee. The young and charismatic priest who lectured her and her companions on the natural methods of family planning gave each of the women a pre-wedding present of a thermometer and a chart so that they could rehearse. Then they had to choose one of six passages from the thoughts of St Paul for the marriage service. She read that wives should be subject to their husbands, and wondered how St Paul's command could accommodate the 'mutual discipline and commitment' required of a couple using the Billings method. The priest thought she was being picky.

The bishop asked husbands to drink less. The woman stayed on the pill.

A pregnant colleague simply lied to the priest about her reasons for wanting to marry at short notice, and she and her intended were excused attendance at the pre-marriage course as the priest thought them 'educated and respectable'. Nothing in her education, even at third level, had opened her mind to contraceptive practice. 'There's a lot of talk, but it's all negative: you don't, you can't, you shouldn't, and taking protective measures is such a conspicuous thing to do.'

'You'd think,' says Marguerite Egan of the Tralee women's group, 'that we were looking for explosives.'

Sexual relations in the Kingdom acquired an illicit, sometimes gleefully illicit, aura as the people set about subverting the dictates of priest, politician and medical practitioner. The most common means of subversion was via the country's internal postal system and the country's only tabloid Sunday paper, whose logo 'Are you getting it every Sunday?' is always displayed on page one above a sub-pornographic picture of an almost naked woman. By the simple means of filling in a cut-out coupon and sending it to the recommended address, readers could obtain by return post as many condoms as they wished, no questions asked about age or marital status. It was entirely illegal but the government of the day turned a gratefully blind eye.

It was not always successful, because other moral police officers were at work, in the person of the village postmistress or postmaster. The package would sometimes arrive steamed open, clumsily resealed and empty, no questions asked, no response expected.

It is difficult in the confined closely knit communities of rural Ireland to sustain an absolutely private life. A Kerrywoman's explanation of her nineteen-year-old daughter's inhibitions about natural bodily functions was illuminating. When the daughter used to go to the crossroads store for sanitary towels the man behind the counter would cheerfully remark 'It's your time again' or 'Safe for another month anyway.'

Such affronts to modesty were as nothing compared to what was said in Kerry, and throughout Ireland, as the Eighties opened. Despite the constitutional aspirations about the rightful place of Irishwomen, they had begun to take their place in the paid workforce, were asserting their sexual freedom and were paying a painful price in the absence of contraceptive protection. The number of children born outside of marriage had risen from 1,709 in 1970 to 3,723 in 1980. The number of women seeking abortion in England had shot up from 1,421 in 1974 to 3,673 in 1983. A minuscule feminist group started campaigning for the right to abortion in Ireland. Abortion was illegal, the group's chances of persuading the public to support the aim were remote in the extreme, but fears of a plot to roll in another constitutional Trojan horse were suddenly expressed by an equally minuscule group of eleven gynaecologists and obstetricians.

The fundamentalist backlash against feminism, which had begun in America when women there won a constitutional right to abortion in 1973, had finally crossed the Atlantic and hit Ireland. We were about to be force-fed a diet of fertilised eggs, embryos and fearsome stories of murder in the womb.

6. Church and State

Joanne Hayes's three pregnancies, conceived between April 1981 and August 1983, occurred at a time of great convulsion in the world that Irishmen ruled. Government changed three times in that period. Each government was dominated by one single issue: abortion. The 'pro-life amendment campaign' was launched in June 1981 and continued until its successful climax in September 1983 when article 7 was added to the Constitution:

> The State acknowledges the right to life of the unborn, and, with due regard to the equal right to life of the mother, guarantees in its laws to respect, and, as far as practicable, by its laws to defend and vindicate that right.

The campaign received the forceful, full-throated and full--hearted backing of the Roman Catholic Church, which claimed a ninety-five per cent membership among the population of the Republic. Its particular champion was Kevin McNamara, bishop of Kerry, who was afterwards promoted by Pope John Paul to the archbishopric of Dublin, the largest Catholic diocese in the whole of Europe.

When the votes were cast to amend the Constitution so that abortion would for all time be prohibited in Ireland, Kerry's 'pro-life' vote was fifty per cent higher than that cast countrywide. This was, on its face, a tribute to the people of that county. Kerry is deeply religious and the people desired deeply to be good. Behind them lay a long tradition of obedience to the faith and sacrifice and martyrdom to its cause.

There had once been as many monastic settlements in the county as there are today multinational factories. Ireland, on the western edge of Europe, had been the cradle of early Christian civilisation, from the fifth to the eighth century, and within those monasteries a lifestyle was developed which gave Ireland the reputation of a 'land of saints and scholars'. All the wards in the Kerry county hospital are named after local monasteries. The maternity wards, gynaecological and obstetrical, are called Gallarus, Ardfert and Clonfert. Of Gallarus oratory the poet Seamus Heaney wrote:

> You can still feel the community pack
> This place: it's like going into a turfstack,
> A core of old dark walled up with stone
> A yard thick. When you're in it alone
> You might have dropped, a reduced creature
> To the heart of the globe. No worshipper
> Would leap up to his God off this floor.
>
> Founded there like heroes in a barrow.
> They sought themselves in the eye of their King
> Under the black weight of their own breathing.
> And how he smiled on them as out they came,
> The sea a censer, and the grass a flame.
>
> from *Door into the Dark* (Faber, 1969), p. 22

Bishop McNamara put his people at the heart of the globe, calling on them to show the way forward once more to a world collapsing under the black weight of murdered babies, which is how he represented abortion. A 'yes' vote in the referendum to amend the Constitution 'will be a vote that some unborn children be not put to death, but allowed to be born', he instructed them. 'The Catholic people will be guided by their Church,' said Denis Foley, their Fianna Fáil representative in the Dáil (parliament).

Two of the three county newspapers put their full weight behind the campaign. *The Kingdom* reproduced on its front page a diagram of the foetus at various stages of development, from one-quarter of an inch long at three weeks until twenty-eight weeks, when its eyes opened, accompanied by the warning that 'social abortion is allowed up to this time in Britain'. The diagram came complete with descriptions of the abortion process. Dilation and curettage required the insertion of a knife 'to cut the child to pieces'. The suction method 'crushes' parts of the baby 'to death'. The saline injection 'burns the outer layers of the child's skin and injects poison', leaving the baby in the womb to die 'now or an hour or two later'. With the hysterectomy method, 'almost all are born alive and most die of exposure'. In Germany, it was asserted, three out of every four babies in the womb were 'terminated'. It must have seemed, and indeed Bishop Cassidy asserted, that the most dangerous place in the world for a baby was in its mother's womb. During those years of pregnancy for Joanne Hayes, with government gone out of control and Catholic supremacy rampant, women's sexuality and fertility was a subject of fear, loathing and hypocrisy.

Kerrymen, saying not a word about contraception, stampeded to the rescue of the eggs which they might have fertilised. The county hosted the inaugural meeting of the Irish Association of Lawyers for the Defence of the Unborn, which stated that 'the debate is as much about the preservation of a Christian civilisation as it is about the unborn'. A woman, said a supportive editorial in *The Kerryman*, 'could now go to a semen bank and select the seed which will give her the perfect child'. Joanne Hayes was then, in February 1983, six months pregnant by Jeremiah Locke, whose wife was also pregnant.

One of these lawyers, Robert Pierse, was invited to give the sermon at Sunday Mass in the north Kerry Church of Ballyduff. 'Country people,' explained Father John Daly, who vacated the pulpit, 'need to have quite a lot of things explained to them. They are very busy and don't have time to read newspapers carefully.' In a Tralee church, Father Martin Hegarty added a new weekly prayer for Sundays: 'We pray that all people will recognise and respect the sacredness of life and that the right to life of the unborn child will always be safe-guarded in our laws. Lord hear us.'

In August 1983, *The Kerryman* reported that 'The chairmen of all local authorities in Kerry have declared themselves pro-life'. In that month Joanne Hayes became pregnant for a third time by Jeremiah Locke, whose wife was also pregnant again. The Kerry branch of the Society for the Protection of the Unborn Child (SPUC) declared that the intra-uterine device and the low-oestrogen pill both worked by 'killing the new human being about one week after conception'. The refer-endum, said Bishop McNamara in that month, was 'a life-and-death issue'. Both women, however, were to bring Jeremiah Locke's babies safely out of the womb.

Fifty of 'Kerry's leading sportsmen pledge their support for the pro-life amendment campaign', announced *The Kerryman*, and 'ten of them are all-Ireland captains'. Also included were the rugby international Moss Keane, a cyclist and a golfer.

Charlie Haughey, who was against contraception for single people then and now, and against abortion for anyone, came to Kerry during the campaign to commemorate the life and death of a party member who had fought with the IRA in the 1916 Rising. 'To this day the daring exploits and brave deeds which he undertook are recounted in song and story and will forever provide a glorious chapter in the story of Kerry's con-tribution to the fight to establish a free, independent Irish Republic.' The man of whom he spoke used to kill people.

The Kerry branch of the Irish Farmers' Association (IFA) called for the resignations of eleven members of the IFA who had expressed opposition to the pro-life campaign, and a Kerry priest congratulated them.

The Irish Medical Association (IMA) came to Killarney for its annual conference in April 1983 and invited Bishop McNamara to address them at a Mass. He warned them against allowing abortion in the 'hard cases' of rape, incest and deformity, saying this would open the 'floodgates' for the pro-abortionists. No woman need fear death as a direct result of pregnancy because 'it is indeed one of the great achievements of the Irish medical profession, an achievement one records with pride and satisfaction, to have shown that, with proper care and determination to respect innocent life in every case, it is never necessary, as a means of saving the mother's life, to take the life of her unborn child'. In Drogheda, on the east coast, Sheila Hodgers and her baby had just died. Radium treatment for the cancer the mother suffered had been ruled out as it would harm the foetus. Her husband used to hear her screams as he crossed the hospital yard. Mother and baby died within hours of the birth, on 19 March 1983.

After the conference, seventy-one of the ninety medical practitioners in Kerry backed the pro-life campaign, stating that 'from a medical point of view, human life begins at the moment of conception and is therefore always entitled to the full protection of the law and of the Constitution from that time'.

Signatories to the statement included every doctor then working in Kerry who was subsequently to testify to the Kerry babies tribunal: Mr John Creedon, consultant obstetrician; Mr Bob McEneaney, consultant psychiatrist; Dr R.F. Chute, GP; Dr Aidan Daly, GP; Dr Liam Hayes, GP; Dr Áine O'Sullivan, GP.

The doctors spoke again on the eve of the vote, adding to their list of seventy-one the names of three more who did not wish their absence, due to holidays, from the original list to be misconstrued as anti-amendment. The doctors were now explicit about where they stood:

> The pro-life amendment campaign is necessary to protect unborn babies from legal abortion. Further, we support the university professors of obstetrics and gynaecology in Dublin, Cork and Galway, and the distinguished team of

jurists who have confirmed that the purpose of the amendment will not alter medical practice as it now exists. We agree and we confirm that no pregnant woman will be put at risk as a result of the adoption of the amendment.

The Kerryman published a thought . . . 'And oh, dear mom, what right is thine, to kill me on the road to birth?'

The amendment was passed on 7 September 1983. The leader of the Irish Labour Party, and Tánaiste (second-in-command) in the coalition government with Fine Gael, Dick Spring, who was one of the few public figures in Kerry to oppose the amendment, commented that it 'enshrined in the Constitution an attitude to women that borders on contempt'.

Marguerite Egan, founder of the minuscule Kerry branch of the anti-amendment campaign, hoped that the people of the county would now turn their attention to the 'abolition of illegitimacy and the introduction of family planning'.

Joanne Hayes was then in the first month of her third pregnancy. Though she visited Dr Liam Hayes regularly to arrange a minor operation for daughter Yvonne's thumb, seeing him the week before she gave birth to the baby that would bring her to police attention, he did not notice that she was carrying an unborn child. His partner, Aidan Daly, who saw Joanne twenty-four hours after she brought that unborn child into the world, did not notice that she had given birth. Mr John Creedon, who did suspect that a baby had been born to her and was now missing, released her from hospital to make her own way in the world. 'I wish someone would define the medical ethics in such a situation', said this man who had signed a petition that bound him to protect the fertilised egg that his co-signer had not noticed.

On 1 May 1984, the police came looking for the woman who had, all unnoticed, brought the baby in her womb through the amendment bushes that the men had been beating. Her women friends had noticed, though.

7. Martina Rohan

I

On the day before Christmas Eve 1983, work finished early at the sports complex and the staff started their ten-day holiday. Most went, as usual, to the Meadowlands hotel, where they met up with workers from the regional technical college, also employed by the local VEC (Vocational Education Committee).

Joanne Hayes, who had not been rostered for work that day, was down town shopping. In the late afternoon she went to the hotel and joined the gang in their celebrations. She had parcels with her. At half past seven Martina Rohan, who shared receptionist duties at the complex with Joanne, left the bar and went to the TV lounge to watch *Coronation Street*, of which she was a fanatic follower. Joanne went with her.

The small TV lounge is an inhospitable place where patrons seldom go. Cream paint on the walls, red drapes and worn red carpet provide perfunctory decoration. A solitary light bulb under a red lampshade throws gloomy illumination on the horse-prints, brass plates and dried ferns in a massive vase. The fireplace is blocked off. Four large uneasy chairs, a sofa and three low formica tables accommodate telly-watchers.

After half an hour of the soap opera, the two women remained in this room and talked about Christmas. Joanne showed Martina the gifts she had bought for her family. There was one extra item in a plastic bag that bore the logo of a men's boutique. The sweater in it was too small, Martina noticed, for Joanne's brothers Ned and Mike. It was for

Jeremiah, Joanne said. Martina asked her how Jeremiah would explain such a generous and personal present to his wife. Joanne replied that he would think of something.

'She's expecting,' said Martina. She doesn't know why – the words just came out. There was something in the nonchalance of Joanne's tone that indicated ignorance of reality.

Joanne 'shot up' in her chair. 'How dare he,' she said. She burst into tears. She gathered her things and left the hotel at once. Martina followed her out to the car park, urging her to come back and talk. It was pouring rain. Joanne was four miles from home, without transport and loaded with parcels. The last bus had long since gone. Joanne asked her to send Jeremiah out.

He was drinking at the bar. He went out to the car park. Ten minutes later he came back. Joanne was not with him. Shortly afterwards the hotel paged him for a phone call. It was Joanne, calling him from a coinbox down the road. He was brief and then he resumed drinking. Joanne hitched home in the wind and the rain and the dark, his present with her.

Martina reproached him. He could at least have driven her back to the farm. He was at first brusque. Then he talked a little. He loved Joanne. He loved his wife, too, 'but in a different way'. Her parents did not approve of the marriage, he said. They were farmers of some substance.

Martina had asked Joanne in the car park to come and visit her over the Christmas break. Joanne did not come. None of her friends in town saw her. The new-year festivities came and went and she did not appear on the social scene. She had begun the deep withdrawal into self-imposed isolation that lasted four months and ended in birth, death and disaster, in the middle of the night, back at the farm out of which she had come six years earlier, at the age of nineteen, to start her promising job in town.

II

The complex opened as a leisure centre in 1977, was quickly successful and began to employ more staff within a year. Joanne and Martina were sent there by Manpower, the state employment agency, in 1978 and they both began work as receptionists the same day. At first acquaintance she always struck strangers as being very tiny. She is four-foot-seven inches tall. She also struck her co-workers, in the beginning, as shy to the point of timidity.

Her previous six-month stint in a Tralee supermarket required of her only that she sit silently at the checkpoint from nine to five punching a cash register, after which she went straight back home. Now she had to receive the public, answer their enquiries, make arrangements for them, mingle with the rest of the staff and work late hours.

Initially, she was only at ease in the company of the children who flocked to the complex. 'If I heard a child cry, I'd run away,' says Martina. 'Joanne would always run towards it, get down on her knees and hug and kiss and chat to the child.'

The atmosphere in the new complex was, they are all agreed, 'fantastic'. There was no manager then. It was run more like a co-operative than anything. People came there to enjoy themselves. It was infectious. The staff enjoyed themselves. It was a hopeful, expanding place to work in, with work to take pride in, and an air of permanence and thriving custom.

The place was frequented by people of all professions and none, old and young, female and male. The unemployed, the mothers and fathers, the guards and solicitors, the doctors and labourers, the white-collared and blue-collared, mingled together. When their clothes came off, for the swimming pool or sauna or gymnasium or sports pitches, they were equal.

Martina Rohan, Aileen Enright, Mary Murphy and Joanne Hayes were all young single women. At first the three townies used to go off together after work for a drink and a bit of *craic*. They had the homes of their parents to go back to, work to look forward to and spare money in their pockets. After a while, Joanne did not automatically return to the farm each evening. She began to hang out with them, not saying much, but eagerly tagging along. Sometimes, when spirits were high, she'd roll down the window of whatever car they found themselves in and yell out to pedestrians. There were pubs and discos and bright lights and fast-food places for their entertainment.

There were, invariably, drinks after work. The timeless, worldwide, men-only ritual of the bar had succumbed in the Sixties to an influx of spending single women, and then married women, who also felt thirsty after a day's paid labour, and who mingled freely with single and married men.

Martin Kennedy, lawyer for the garda superintendents, was to express shock during the tribunal that these women would one day attend when he heard that Peggy Houlihan, a married woman who worked as a cleaner at the complex, engaged in this normal healthy practice. She was recalling an after-work drink with Joanne Hayes and Jeremiah Locke.

'Drinking with a married man. I see,' he declared.

Joanne's women friends noticed, in the beginning, that she did not have many clothes. Her dress was as quiet and unvaried as her lifestyle. When celebration days or birthdays came round, they used to give her presents of fashionable gear. She began to blossom. She became quite assured. She did not stand out in a crowd, but she was no longer invisible.

On the other hand, the women did not always go around in a crowd; nor did they go out together every night. On those mornings when they'd come in, grinning and exhausted, to tell individual tales of the night before and where they'd been and who they'd been with, Joanne would have nothing to say. If she had not been with them, she had been at the farm, watching TV and reading her favourite magazine, *True Romance*.

Her social life effectively consisted of drinks after work at the Meadowlands. Jeremiah Locke used to be there. He was one of the few with a car. If the drinking developed into a prolonged session, he'd drop Martina off at her house and give Joanne a lift out to the farm.

He was on sufficiently friendly terms with the women to invite them to drop in at the reception which followed his wedding in 1981. Martina Rohan was working late, but Joanne and Aileen Enright, who both finished at three that afternoon, called into the reception and joined in the singing and dancing and drinking. Jeremiah kissed all the women goodbye as he set off on his honeymoon. Shaking hands died out decades ago. Even the priest kisses the bride. So Jeremiah kissed Aileen and Joanne and the others and went away with his wife.

His marriage was barely six months old when Joanne started coming in to work in the mornings with her own stories of where she'd been the night before, but she never said who she'd been with. Her friends didn't ask. They knew. They also knew not to ask. It was fairly unspeakable.

Joanne Hayes remembers the night she and Jeremiah Locke became lovers. It was 26 October, a bank holiday, she was to tell the tribunal when they insisted on knowing.

She and Jeremiah were not discreet. They engaged in horseplay in the staff canteen, behind the reception area, throwing tea bags and cups of water at each other. They were bringing their private life into the workplace. Jeremiah Locke's wife Mary came to the complex and had a public blazing row in the reception area with Joanne.

There was a certain amount of embarrassment about the situation among her friends. There was quite a lot of anxiety. Martina Rohan spoke her mind just once, at an early stage in the affair. She voiced her opinion on the hopelessness of the relationship, and the hurt to Jeremiah Locke's wife. She was mainly concerned about Joanne, who was still regarded as naive. Joanne cut her off abruptly.

The head of the VEC, John Falvey, sent separately for Joanne and Jeremiah to express concern. The sports complex

was not a normal business enterprise and its viability depended on relationships with the public. The relationship
between Joanne and Jeremiah was becoming scandalously
public. Both denied it.

Martina Rohan was becoming anxious for other reasons.
Both women were employed in a temporary capacity, on contracts that were renewed every six months, with the promise
held out that one day they'd be made permanent. They
appealed without success to their union and to Dick Spring of
the Labour Party to fight for their job security. Now Mr Falvey
began to send regular letters to them both, reminding them
that they were temporary workers, hinting that the contracts
might not be renewed. There was a recession, after all. Or was
this a warning shot across the bows?

On one occasion, after receiving such letters, both women
became highly agitated. They went to the Meadowlands and
talked the situation over. That evening stands out in both their
minds. A job, in the early Eighties, was worth its weight in
gold. Martina's father had been made redundant and she and
her sister were the only wage-earners in the household. Joanne
was the only wage-earner in hers.

That was when Joanne was pregnant with Yvonne.

In February 1984, when Joanne was again visibly pregnant,
she and Martina were called to an interview board. One of
them would be given a permanent job.

Martina got the job. She was not a mother.

Joanne's temporary contract would be reviewed when the
time came. Her chances of renewal must have appeared slight,
because to the outsider her relationship with Jeremiah must
have seemed as ongoing as her pregnancies.

'When I didn't get that permanent job I felt bitter. I think I
didn't get it because I was pregnant again,' she was to say in a
private conversation during the tribunal hearings. She had just
gone through a bitter day in the witness box, but she hadn't
told how she had felt in that month of February, pregnant,

abandoned by her lover and facing unemployment. Nor did she tell them that her regraded job had been advertised on 6 April. In any case, the lawyers were too busy castigating her for that night of 13 April on the farm. They were interested in the moments after birth, not the long period of gestation. The fertilised egg had survived its time in the womb, after all.

On Tuesday 1 May Martina Rohan left home to work the 3 pm-to-10 pm shift. On her way to the complex a workmate pulled up alongside her on a bicycle. He wanted to give her a lift on his crossbar. She laughed him off but he insisted that there was something she ought to know. As the bicycle carried them both away from the kerb, he said that the Special Branch police were waiting for her up at the office. They wanted to interview her. 'Joanne has been arrested,' he said. 'They've got her down at the station for the Cahirciveen baby.'

She remembers that the whole frame of the bike began to shake.

She remembers the previous weekend. Joanne had come into the complex with a doctor's sick certificate that explained her fortnight's absence from work. She would be resuming work on Monday, she said. She propped Yvonne up on the counter. She said she had been in hospital with a miscarriage. Why hadn't she told her pals, Martina wanted to know. They would have come to visit her. That was a terrible thing to go through alone. Did Jeremiah know? He didn't. She asked Joanne if she would like Martina to tell him. Joanne didn't want him to know. She began to cry.

On Monday, at work, Joanne had been quiet and miserable. On Tuesday she was in the police station and two detectives were waiting for Martina. The two men made jokes about the way she was frantically smoking. There was no need to worry, they said. The Cahirciveen baby was mentioned almost immediately. 'There's no way Joanne would do that. You've got the wrong woman,' Martina said. They said they just wanted to know about Joanne anyway. She told them that her workmates knew she was pregnant, that she had resisted all conversation about it and that she had lost the baby only a fortnight ago.

One of them wrote down her words and then put the written sheets of paper in front of her, requesting her signature on them. 'I suppose I'm signing my life away,' she said. 'Not to worry,' they said. She didn't read the statement.

That night she went to the house of Mary Murphy, now O'Riordan, and the two of them talked and talked.

8. Mary O'Riordan

Mary Murphy, a lifeguard in the complex, had been the first person there to ask Joanne if she was pregnant with Yvonne. It had been commonly voiced but never confirmed, because no one had ever spoken to her about it. When Mary returned from her honeymoon with husband John and heard the rumour, she decided to talk to her. She said straight out that everyone was saying Joanne was pregnant. 'Is it true, girl?' she asked.

'Oh thank God you've said it Murph. I was dying for someone to know. I've no one to talk to.' Joanne was then about five months pregnant. The two women became close. Mary had never much been a feature of the social scene, having a steady boyfriend. Anyway, she says, looking back on her life at twenty-one, she only drank coffee then.

Joanne's family was reticent about the impending birth. There was embarrassment and stiffness and worry in the house. Shortly after Yvonne was born, Mary went out to Abbeydorney and the family was still distinctly uneasy, not knowing how to introduce the child.

Mary O'Riordan did not afterwards discuss contraception with her friend. Joanne was, after all, then twenty-three years of age, and no longer an unschooled girl in from the country. She had already had a baby. 'That's a hard knock to get. You assume a woman doesn't take chances after that. And you'd assume that Jeremiah . . .'

It came as a revelation to Mary O'Riordan in any case, in the course of the tribunal, that Joanne and Jeremiah had actually been having a regular, long-standing relationship. 'I thought she'd only been with him a couple of times. That they'd begun as friends, wandered into it and wandered out again.' On the rare occasions during the pregnancy with Yvonne when Joanne's relationship with Jeremiah had been raised, the conversation had been brief. Joanne did not wish to talk about it. Mary thought they'd been having a 'now you've learned your lesson about going out with married men' discussion, even though Joanne declared affection for him still.

Mary had pointed out the hurt to the feelings of Jeremiah's wife. Joanne had countered that the marriage was over, resisting responsibility. Mary had cautioned that he was still with his wife, scarcely evidence of a commitment now to Joanne. Joanne had shrugged her shoulders. The conversations were as brief as that, and so, Mary thought, had been Joanne's affair with Jeremiah.

Increasingly their conversation had been about babies. Mary's first baby was due in December, five months after Yvonne. When she took maternity leave from the complex she did not know that Joanne was pregnant once more. While Mary O'Riordan was giving birth, Joanne was learning that Mary Locke was as pregnant as she was.

A woman who wrote to Joanne during the subsequent tribunal brought imaginative empathy to bear on that situation: 'I used to think you didn't care about the baby you killed. Now I know, after thinking about you, and living with you through those hours on the witness stand, that you hadn't a baby at all, you had a pregnancy. It's not the same thing.'

After the birth of her son Wayne, Mary O'Riordan decided to take a year off work. Her contact with Joanne was sporadic and usually by telephone through the winter. 'Joanne didn't come to my house to see my baby.' As the spring of 1984 approached, she heard for the first time of Joanne's condition. 'We talked about it when we finally met. She was wondering about a flat in Tralee, with the cheap council rent for unmarried mothers, and the allowance and the free milk.'

It was by no means a secret pregnancy. It was common knowledge at the complex, though there was no sense of urgency. 'Talk of doctors, booking into hospital, telling her family, that was all in the future,' says Mary. 'You take things with Joanne in stages. It was nowhere near that stage. She was miserable and withdrawn. I was standing by.'

Then she got a call. Joanne rang up to say that she had been in hospital, that the baby had miscarried. 'I was puzzled. We met and sat out in my back garden. I said "How could a baby miscarry at seven or eight months?" I was wondering rather than questioning. Joanne was sad, and I was sad for the loss of the baby. It was that kind of wondering.'

In that atmosphere of sadness Mary did not press for details, nor did she ask how in God's name Joanne did not know whether the miscarried child was a girl or a boy. 'Anyway, I never got a good run at the subject with her, though we sat out on the grass from one in the afternoon till eight in the evening. Women kept calling at the house.' In that young, upwardly mobile, thriving housing estate, the new mothers spent much time calling on each other, sharing the work of child-rearing.

Mary drove Joanne home that night, delivering her to a farmhouse that was full, she said, of shy disquieted people. There was sadness and disturbance and reticence everywhere in the family.

The next week, on 1 May, towards three in the afternoon, the guards called at Mary's house. They were in civilian clothes. Her son needed a change of nappy. He did not get it for another hour. Joanne, the guards said, had had a baby and they wanted to know a few things. Cahirciveen was never mentioned and Mary in fact asked most of the questions. 'Why are you asking me about Joanne? What do you have to do with her? She miscarried her baby and if you want to know more, shouldn't you ring the hospital?'

When the guards left, Mary rang the sports complex to

speak to Joanne. Irene McGaley told her that Joanne was down in the station answering for the Cahirciveen baby. Later that day, Martina Rohan called to her house. They talked in puzzled circles, mainly to the effect that the guards were 'out of their trees'. Around 10 pm they drove down by the station and around it, again and again, puzzled beyond comprehension, wondering was she in there, unable to do anything, not knowing what to do about their friend who had miscarried in hospital and was facing accusations of stabbing a baby to death, which they knew she was totally incapable of.

Towards midnight, Mary's husband Tom, who sells life insurance to the guards, rang the station and the police told him that Joanne was to be charged with the murder of the Cahirciveen baby.

Next morning Mary went to court. She found a seat beside Kathleen Hayes.

'Kathleen, what in God's name is going on?'

'I don't know, I'm not sure. They say Joanne killed a baby, and I'm going out to Abbeydorney now to look for it.'

Look for what? Mary thought this whole family had gone funny in the head. Joanne was brought down a corridor in the company of a ban gharda (policewoman). Mary stepped forward. Joanne looked up – she always has to look up to six-foot Mary – her eyes full of tears, but she registered no impression at the sight of her friend. 'She was in a totally different world by then.'

On the six-o'clock radio news Mary heard that 'an unknown infant' had been found at Abbeydorney. 'I knew more than the newsreader at that stage. I knew from Kathleen that this was Joanne's baby. Now I was totally confused. I didn't know what to make of anything. She hadn't stabbed the Cahirciveen baby, but a baby turns up on her farm that I thought she had miscarried in hospital.'

Two weeks later, when Joanne had been released from the mental hospital to which she had been transferred from

Limerick prison, she rang Mary and they went out together. 'We spent the summer going out together. I'd arrange a babysitter or put Wayne in the baby-seat in the back of the car, drive out to the farm, pick her up and we'd go driving round. They wouldn't say much to me in the farmhouse. I'd arrive, say are you ready, she'd say she was ready and off we'd go, driving round and round, talking about nothing really. Joanne didn't want to talk about what had happened.'

The friendship between these two women survived the endless hours of meaningless small talk as they drove round literally, and conversationally drove round, the abyss that had opened up under the feet of the Hayes family. 'She wouldn't talk about the birth or the baby she'd had. She'd talk a lot about the guards, ask her anything you like about those twelve hours in the garda station and she'd frighten you with a description of what went on in there, but about that night in Abbeydorney, nothing.'

Sometimes Mary would blurt out, 'But what was it like, giving birth in a field? Why did you? Were you out of your mind? Why didn't you call for somebody?' Joanne would always reply that it happened so quickly, a few minutes of labour . . . she'd get tense and distressed and they'd veer away from the subject, driving round and round the countryside.

At the tribunal, lawyers were to make much of the fact that neither Joanne Hayes nor her family had talked throughout the summer to their solicitor about garda brutality to them. They didn't ask Joanne's women friends if she had talked to them about it. The women were asked only what they knew about Joanne's pregnancies and her love-life. The guards had been very interested in that, too, when they interviewed her and her family.

9. Behind Closed Doors

I

The police had not come for the Hayes family early in the morning on 1 May. People on the dole and pension do not have to rise at dawn. It was assumed that Joanne would still be on sick pay. Detectives Gerry O'Carroll and P.J. Browne waited in a car on the main road outside the farm to watch the family drive down to the village to sign on at the garda station for their state benefits.

Ned and Kathleen drove out alone shortly after ten. Below in the village, hidden in a room behind the public area, waited extra guards, specially drafted into the one-man police station for the occasion.

The Hayeses saw all the garda cars in the street. After doing their business they returned to the farm. Guard Liam Moloney drove up after them, asked where Joanne was and heard that she was at work. He left, saying he'd be back later. Shortly after midday, two detectives went to the sports complex, found Joanne and brought her down to Tralee station. At the same time four garda cars swept into the Hayes farmyard. Detectives got out and some spoke with Ned and Mike, who had come out to see them, some spoke to Aunt Bridie at the back door and others went inside the house.

Kathleen was interviewed in the kitchen and her mother was brought into the disused parlour that lies between the kitchen and the bathroom. After an hour Kathleen was allowed to serve up the dinner. Bridie was missing. She went out to the yard to call Ned and Mike and discovered that they weren't there.

Aunt Bridie, Ned and Mike had been taken to Tralee garda station. Kathleen and her mother ate their meal, then Kathleen gave cups of tea to the detectives, after which she was brought to Abbeydorney garda station. She was later transferred to Tralee garda station.

Her mother was left alone in the farmhouse with Yvonne, not yet a year old, and two detectives. Eventually she would be left totally alone with the baby, and she would not see the other members of the family until half past one the following morning. She could not drive and there was no telephone in the house. Guard Liam Moloney had arranged that two male neighbours would milk the cows while the Hayeses were being questioned in various locations, and the sight of the police posted at the gate daunted would-be visitors.

The only clues available to the police when they started to interview the family were the information that the hospital had doubts about Joanne, and the assumption that the Cahirciveen baby had fallen out of a brown plastic bag which was inside a torn fertiliser bag. The 0-7-30 fertiliser bag was one of a batch of two hundred thousand.

Initially every single member of the family denied that Joanne had been pregnant. Within half an hour, though, of her first experience of police questioning, Joanne stopped the denials. She told Guard Moloney that she had given birth in a field and concealed the baby's body. She was greeted with incredulity and the Dublin detectives were brought in.

She told them that she had miscarried and flushed the miscarriage down the toilet. Gerry O'Carroll said that, if that were so, the foetus would still be in the septic tank. Joanne then told them exactly where the baby was hidden, out on the farm.

Two guards who were sent out to search for it came back saying they had found nothing.

Ned was next to start talking, elsewhere in the station, around 2.30 pm. 'Whatever happened, happened in the house,' he said. He had slept up in the cottage. He knew, he said, that Joanne had had a baby, but did not know where it was, and he thought Kathleen and Mike had taken it away.

Then he started making an admission that placed a stabbed baby in a fertiliser bag that was marked 0-7-30. Detective Dillon produced to him the 0-7-30 bag in which the Cahirciveen baby had been found and he agreed that it was similar to the one he had used. He had tossed the bag off the cliffs of Slea Head, standing at the outer edge of a peninsula which is separated by eleven miles of water from the opposite peninsula, around the corner of which is Cahirciveen.

Mike started agreeing, around four o'clock, that Joanne had had a baby. He did not know where it was, he said, because he thought Kathleen and Ned had taken it away. Then he started making a confession that placed a baby, which had been stabbed with a kitchen knife, in a manure bag in the water off Slea Head.

Their mother insisted, in a five-o'clock statement, that Joanne had miscarried in hospital and then guards arrived to make a forensic examination of Joanne's bedroom. Guard Liam Moloney spoke with one of the men interviewing Mary Hayes. Detectives Coote and Smith were new to the Cahirciveen case, having missed the conference the night before. They had driven other detectives out to the farm at noon and had been left behind with the mother and grand-child, Yvonne. After speaking with Guard Moloney the detectives took a second statement from Mary Hayes at six o'clock. Joanne's mother now placed a baby, beaten to death with a toilet brush, in a turf bag that Ned and Mike had taken away. She did not mention stabbing.

Detectives Smith and Coote took a turf bag, bath brush and carving knife from her home and brought them into Tralee station along with the confession.

Joanne was apprised of her mother's second statement at eight o'clock and now she, too, changed her original state-ment. She placed the birth in her bedroom, and the corpse in a turf bag which Ned and Mike took away. She had beaten the baby with the very bath brush and stabbed it with the very knife which the detectives showed her.

While Joanne was making this statement Detective Smith moved on with the carving knife to the room where Kathleen was still denying all knowledge of a birth. Shortly after nine o'clock he and guard Liam Moloney took from Kathleen a statement which had herself and Ned and Mike taking the stabbed baby away in a turf bag which was thrown into the water at Slea Head.

Joanne was brought downstairs to talk with Bridie towards 10 pm, after which Bridie made and signed a statement in which she had helped deliver a live child about whose fate she knew nothing more.

The state solicitor, Donal Browne, was called to the station as Bridie was speaking. After reading the typed statements of Joanne, her mother and Mike, and listening to a summary of the others, he recommended that charges be brought. A local peace commissioner convened a midnight court in the station and the family was arraigned before him, one by one, and charged.

Joanne was accused of murdering the Cahirciveen baby, and the others accused of concealment of its birth. The guards felt that they could always charge the mother, Mary Hayes, who was still out at the farmhouse, on another day. There would be time enough for that.

II

Joanne's initial confessions on that Mayday were as follows:

> Date: 1/5/84.   Tralee Garda Station.
> Interview commenced: 12.35 pm.
> Present: Ban gharda Ursula O'Regan. Garda Liam Moloney.
>   Memo of interview with Joanne Hayes, after
>   caution.

Admission: 1.25 pm: 'I had the baby boy at home. I delivered the baby myself on the
12/4/84. I panicked and hid it. The
baby is dead, I buried it at home.'

After caution, 1.35 pm:

'On Thursday night 12/4/84 sometime around half-
eleven or twelve o'clock, I gave birth to a baby boy of six to
seven months in a field at my brother's farm. I delivered
the baby myself with my own hands. I delivered the baby
standing up. I panicked and then I put the baby down on
some hay. I went in home and said nothing. I went to bed
and couldn't sleep. I got up at 5 am, I sat down and had
some tea and went back to bed until 7.30 am.

'I got up and went out to the baby. I put my baby into a
blue and white plastic bag. I think it was a bag from
O'Carroll's chemists, Tralee. I then put the baby into a
brown paper bag first and then into the plastic bag, I mean.
I put the baby down in the river, it's a pool of water.'

Relevant extracts from all subsequent incriminating statements
are given below.

Ned Hayes said:

I went to bed straight away after going home and I was
reading a book called The Great Hunger until about
twelve midnight. I turned off the light and fell asleep.

Sometime during the night, around 2.30 am, I would
think, I was awakened by my sister Kathleen knocking on
the front room window where I sleep. She asked me to
come down quick. She sounded excited and she left.

I got up, had a drink of water and went down to the
farmhouse after about fifteen minutes.

I met my mother walking out the boreen outside the
house to meet me. She said that we had big trouble here
at the moment.

She told me that Joanne was after having a child and
that she, Joanne was after doing away with the child. She
was crying and looked very upset.

We went into the kitchen and my brother and sister Kathleen were inside. The two of them were bawling crying and they were very upset.

I was shattered and I was shaking all over.

I sat on a chair beside the table with my back to all the bedrooms. I took a drink of orange to cool my nerves.

I went up into Joanne's room. I met my Aunt Bridie just coming out of the room. She was crying and shaking all over.

I stood at the door of the room.

I saw Joanne lying on the bed with just a nightdress on. I saw the body of a newly born child at the foot of the bed.

I have drawn a sketch of the room and what I saw when I went into the room.

Ned Hayes drew a sketch for the guards that showed his sister Joanne in the bed, at the foot of which was a baby.

The infant was lying face downwards naked on the bed. I said to my sister 'Why in fuck's name did you do it?' I said to her that surely we could have kept the child and reared it.

She did not answer as she was crying away.

I went away from the door and went back up a couple of minutes afterwards. I repeated what I said the first time and she said that she didn't want to bring shame on the family. She said that six months ago Locke said they would go away together and set up house.

I went back down to the kitchen where there was a cup of tea ready. We all had tea. There wasn't a word spoken about it.

I went out for a breath of fresh air for about ten minutes and when I came back in, my mother suggested that we would have to get some way of getting rid of it. We talked for about three-quarters of an hour of getting rid of it.

I was in favour of burying it on the land, but my mother and Aunt Bridie weren't in favour of it. Aunt Bridie was in favour of us throwing it in the sea.

My brother and I went outside to get a plastic bag. My brother picked up a plastic bag from the gable end of the house. I shone a torch for him to find it. The bag had some sand in it for putting on top of silage. He emptied out the sand.

We went into the kitchen and up into Joanne's room.

I emptied out a brown plastic shopping bag of clothes which I found beside the shopping bag in the room.

We caught a leg each of the infant and put it head first into the brown shopping bag.

As we lifted the dead infant I could see blood on its chest. It was stabbed in the chest. I couldn't see how many wounds were in the chest.

When we had placed the dead infant in the brown plastic bag, Joanne asked to be left alone in the room with the child for a few minutes.

Both of us went back to the kitchen and left her alone for about ten minutes. We laid the bag containing the infant on the floor beside the bed.

When we returned to the room, she was on the bed turned towards the wall. The brown bag had been rolled closed so that the infant was not visible. We opened the grey fertiliser bag – which was an 0-7-30 – wider, and each caught an end of the brown bag and put it into the grey bag. I have on this date been shown a grey fertiliser bag 0-7-30 and a brown shopping bag by Detective Sergeant Dillon and they are similar to the ones we used that morning.

When we had placed the brown bag with the infant into the grey bag, my sister Joanne asked again to be left alone with the infant. We again placed it on the floor and left for about two minutes.

When we returned she was in a similar position facing the wall and the top of the grey bag was tied with a string.

I caught hold of the top of the bag and Michael caught the bottom of the bag. We took it through the kitchen.

My sister Kathleen had the door of the car open as I had already asked her. Kathleen had the keys of the car and she handed me the keys of the car afterwards. I placed the bag on the floor of the car behind the driver's seat. The car is the property of my Aunt Bridie but both Michael and myself are insured to drive it.

I went back into the house and brought a road map with me. I went back into the kitchen and told my mother and aunt that we were leaving. My sister Kathleen had gone down into Joanne's room where she was sleeping on a mattress.

I drove the car and my brother accompanied me in the front passenger seat of the car which is a two-door. We brought a shovel with us in case we might get a place to bury it.

We fully intended when we left the house that we would go to the sea with the bag and the further away the better. I drove the car into Tralee, on to Blennerville, out the Dingle Road. At Camp Cross I stopped and took out the map to decide which road we would go. We decided to go by Conor Pass as we thought it would be the quietest.

Going up Conor Pass we stopped for about three minutes and looked at the map to decide which way we would go. We didn't pick out any place on the map to dispose of the body and we decided to drive on for another bit.

We went on into Dingle and went out the Ventry Road. We stopped this side of Ventry and looked at the map again.

It was then we decided to go to Slea Head.

We drove on until we came to a spot about two miles on the Ventry side of Slea Head. I am familiar with Ventry and Slea Head as I have been there on a number of occasions. When I got to this spot which I thought was the most suitable place I got out of the car and I took out the bag containing the body. I walked around the back of the car with the bag and opened the door for my brother. I asked my brother to keep a watch out and I went in over a stone ditch, walked about twenty yards to the edge of the cliff.

I flung the bag from the cliff and into the sea. I would say there was a drop of about ten feet and I watched the bag drop directly into the water.

I returned to the car, turned the car about on the roadway and drove back the same way as we had come. We arrived back in Abbeydorney about 10 am.

The mother and the sister Kathleen met us outside the door and I told them where I had disposed of the bag and its contents.

Mary Hayes said:

I remember Tuesday night 10 April, 1984 at 7 pm. I knew Joanne my daughter was ill as she was losing a lot of blood around and I knew she was about to have a baby.

At about 2.30 am the following morning 11/4/84 Joanne had a baby in her room.

Bridie, Mike and Kathleen was with her.

After the child was born Mike and Kathleen came down from Joanne's room to tell me in the kitchen about the birth of the child and they left Bridie alone with Joanne.

About five minutes later Bridie came down to the kitchen to tell me to go down quick and see the child and Joanne, Kathleen and Mike came with me and in the bedroom I saw Joanne lying in her bed and the baby was at the bottom of the bed.

I saw that the baby was dead and its body was marked.

I saw a white toilet brush beside the bed and Joanne used that brush to beat the child.

I then left with Kathleen to call my other son Ned who was in bed above in our other house which is about 100 yards away.

Before I left to go up for Ned, Joanne was crying out aloud and was very upset. I saw her with the toilet brush in her hand.

When I arrived back down with Ned, Joanne had calmed back down.

I said to Joanne 'You will have to bury the child' and Mike or Kathleen said we will bury the child on the land.

I said the child cannot be buried on the land. Ned and Mike went to the back kitchen where they got a turf bag and put the child into the bag. I told Mike and Ned that they would have to bury the child. They left, Mike and Ned, with the child in the bag and drove out of the yard about 5 am.

They, Mike and Ned, returned at about 7 am and said that they had buried the child. I did not ask them where. We all decided not to talk or tell anybody about it.

Joanne's room was all blood after the birth and when Joanne got up the following day she washed the bed clothes and room.

I have been shown the white toilet brush by Detective Garda Smith and I identified it as the brush Joanne had with her the night the child was born.

I have also been shown a turf bag by Detective Garda Smith and that is similar to the one used by Mike and Ned to take away the baby.

I have been shown a carving knife by Detective Garda Smith and that is the knife we normally carve the meat with.

My husband died on 25/8/1975 and I have brought up my children with the help of my sister Bridie Fuller who has lived with me all her life.

Michael Hayes said:

On the Tuesday night of the week before Easter week myself, Johanna [sic] and Bridie, my aunt, went to bed at about 11.30 pm to three different rooms. Shortly after going to bed I went to sleep. I was awakened at about 2 am to 2.30 am by a person roaring and shouting.

I got up and I heard that the roaring and shouting was coming from Johanna's room. I went into her room. My aunt was there before me standing near the top of Johanna's bed. Siobhan [sic] was in a cot beside the side of the bed. There was a new-born baby on the bed beside Johanna and she had her arm around it. The bedspread was wrapped around the baby. The baby was alive and crying.

I got a shock when I saw another baby there again even though I knew she was expecting.

I stayed a few minutes in the room, I didn't say anything. My aunt was saying something, I don't know what she said. I left my aunt in the room and went out to the kitchen. My sister Kathleen who had stayed in the same room as Johanna was also in the room. My mother, who had slept in the room with me, had gone into Johanna's room before me, and she was also in the room.

I had put on my clothes before leaving my bedroom.

My mother, aunt and sister Kathleen were giving out to her for having this child and going out with a married man. They were cross with her.

I was up and down to the room every couple of minutes. I did this a lot of times. My mother, aunt and Kathleen were in the room all this time.

My mother left the room and went to the kitchen.

Kathleen then brought up a toilet brush from the bathroom, to the bedroom. She gave the brush to Johanna. I was standing at the door. Kathleen went into the kitchen and got a kitchen knife from a cabinet in the kitchen inside the back door. It was a pointed knife, it had a rough blade and brown timber handle and she gave it to Johanna who was inside in bed.

The baby was beside Johanna in the bed.

Johanna stabbed the baby on the chest three times. The bedspread was all blood after.

The baby's face was towards the ceiling and its feet were facing the bottom of the bed.

I stayed standing.

Kathleen was near the bed when Johanna was doing it. Then Johanna got out of bed. I saw her catch hold of the toilet brush in her right hand and she hit the child on the face and body a number of times. The baby was on the floor at this stage as it had fallen off the bed when Johanna was getting out of bed.

Johanna put the baby up on the bed then. The bedspread was still around the baby.

The baby was dead at this stage.

My mother came into the room. Ned my brother came into the bedroom at this stage. My mother said that we'd bury the body in the field, the rest of us said we'd throw it into the sea.

Myself and Ned went out to the back yard.

We got a blue manure bag similar to the one shown me today by Detective Garda John O'Sullivan. We got a big stone which we dug up, and we put it into the bag. I stayed in the yard and Ned went into the house. I then went up to the back door. The light was on in the back kitchen.

Ned came out to the back kitchen with Kathleen and they had the baby wrapped up in a newspaper and a clear plastic bag and a brown shopping bag similar to the two bags shown to me by Detective Garda O'Sullivan.

I held the manure bag and Ned put the baby's body which I saw was a baby boy into the manure bag.

I got a piece of binder twine off a bale of hay in the shed and I tied the top of the bag down about half ways. Ned put it into the boot of our Ford Fiesta car and I sat in the front passenger seat. We didn't know where we would go at that time.

It was about 4.30 am Wednesday morning we drove into Tralee. We went down by the Dingle bridge outside Tralee. We stopped after passing the bridge and Ned took out a map.

We decided to drive down to Dingle.

We went over the mountain road. We went through one village on the way and when we got into Dingle we turned right and we continued straight on until we came to a bridge about a mile from the town. We continued straight on for about seven or eight miles.

We were near the sea then and Ned took the bag with the body in it and he crossed over a field and I saw him throwing the bag containing the baby's body into the sea.

The sun was just rising in the sky then.

I had no watch on me and I don't know what time [it was].

We came back to Tralee by the same road. We got petrol in Tralee at Horan's garage. We drove home then. I had my breakfast and milked the cows and went to the creamery.

We tried to keep it all quiet and it looks like we didn't succeed.

Joanne Hayes said:

My mother and all the lads at home were upset about the first baby, but they accepted it and they decided to help me rear it. They were all very upset when I became pregnant again and I was thoroughly and absolutely ashamed of myself and I tried to hide it. I wore tight clothes and I tried not to let it show.

On the 12–13 April 1984, I was at home in the farmhouse in my own room. The baby, Yvonne, was in the cot. Sometime during the night I started to go into labour and a baby boy was born. I was in my own bed, in my own room, in the old farmhouse.

My Auntie Bridie Fuller was present at the birth and delivered the baby.

Michael, my brother, was in the house at the time.

The baby was alive and crying and my Auntie Bridie placed him at the end of the bed.

She left the room to make a pot of tea and I got up and went to the toilet. On the way back to the bedroom I picked up the white bath brush and I went to the cabinet in the kitchen and picked up the carving knife with the brown timber handle.

These are the items I have been shown here today by Detectives Garda Smith and Coote.

I went back to the bedroom and I hit the baby on the head with the bath brush. I had to kill him because of the shame it was going to bring on the family and because Jeremiah Locke would not run away with me and live with me.

The baby cried when I hit it and I stabbed it with the carving knife on the chest and all over the body. I turned the baby over and I also stabbed him in the back. The baby stopped crying after I stabbed it.

There was blood everywhere on the bed and there was also blood on the floor. I then threw the knife on the floor.

My mother, Auntie Bridie, Kathleen my sister and my two brothers Ned and Mike ran into the bedroom.

I was crying and so was my mother, my sister Kathleen and my Auntie Bridie.

I told them I would have to get rid of the body of the baby and then my two brothers said they would bury it.

I told them they would have to take away the baby from the farmyard and they said they would.

Everyone was panicking at this stage.

The boys then brought in a white plastic bag and they put the baby into it and then they put this bag into a turf bag similar to the one Detectives Smith and Coote showed me earlier on this evening at the station.

The boys then left in our own car with the baby. I heard the car leaving the farmyard.

I was feeling sick and depressed and upset. Soon afterwards the afterbirth came and I put it into a brown bucket beside the bed. I then changed the sheets and I put the bloody sheets on the floor until the following day.

I then took my baby Yvonne into my bed and Bridie remained on in the house.

All the others left and went to our cottage about a hundred yards away.

I got up around 5 am and I took the brown bucket with the afterbirth in it and I went out the front and I put the afterbirth into the old hay beside the well. I went back up to the house and I went to bed again.

I woke up again at about 7.30 am and my brother Michael was back in the house again. I started to clear up my bedroom after that. I gathered up all the sheets that had blood on them, and the brown-handled carving knife and the white bath brush.

I washed the knife and the brush and put them back in

their proper places. I then washed the sheets. Since the night that I killed my baby there was never any talk about it in the house. When the body of the baby was found at Cahirciveen I knew deep down it was my baby.

I was going to call him Shane.

I am awful sorry for what happened, may God forgive me.

Kathleen Hayes said:

Joanne was in her bedroom with Yvonne. My Aunt Bridie was also in bed. I went to Joanne's room and she asked me to change Yvonne's nappy and get her ready for bed. Joanne was standing beside the bed and Yvonne was down on the bed.

I asked my brother Mike who was standing at the door of Joanne's bedroom to hold the baby for a few minutes while I was getting her clothes in the kitchen. When I returned with the baby's clothes, Mike went to bed. The bedroom is next to Joanne's.

My mother went to bed almost immediately after Mike, and Joanne went out the front door. She told me 'I am better off out in the fresh air. I'm walking around all night.'

I knew she was pregnant but I thought she was about seven months pregnant.

When I had finished getting Yvonne ready for bed I put her into Joanne's bed. I then went out the front door at about 12.30 am on Friday 13 April 1984.

I called Joanne. The light outside the front door was on. I could not see her, but she answered my call. She said 'I am all right. I'll be in, in a minute.'

She came in at about 1.15 am, and at this time I was lying inside on Joanne's bed with Yvonne.

I heard Joanne in the kitchen and then I heard her going to the bathroom and locking the door of the bathroom. After about a quarter of an hour she came out of the bathroom.

I had gone from the bedroom to the kitchen and I was talking to Joanne for a minute in the kitchen. She went to bed before me.

When she had left the kitchen I saw drops of blood on the kitchen floor near the hot press.

I then went to Joanne's bedroom. She said to me 'I had a heavy period' and asked me for some towels. I told her I had none.

It was about 1.45 am at this time.

I lay down on the mattress on the floor and Joanne was in bed and Yvonne was inside [sic] her in the bed.

At about 2 am on 13/4/84 Joanne called me and asked me if I was asleep. I answered her.

She said 'I think I am having a baby.'

I got up and I called my Aunt Bridie who came up to Joanne's bedroom. Bridie then called Mom. My brother Mike who is sleeping in the same room as Mom also got up. I took Yvonne from Joanne's bed and put her into her cot. She was asleep when I put her into her cot.

Joanne was having labour pains and Aunt Bridie went to assist Joanne in having the baby. My mother and brother Mike were present in the room when the baby was born.

The baby was crying after birth.

It was a baby boy.

Joanne was upset when the baby was born and she was crying.

I said the baby was 'a fine little lad'.

My Aunt Bridie cut the umbilical cord with a scissors. She placed the baby at the end of the bed on the bed clothes. I went to the kitchen and got a basin of luke-warm water and gave it to my Aunt Bridie. She washed the baby and washed Joanne. There was blood on the sheets on the bed.

My mother, my brother Mike was also present when the baby was born.

My mother was upset and she said 'One of his children was enough to have,' meaning Jeremiah Locke.

I took the basin of water down to the kitchen and when I returned Aunt Bridie was gone to her room and my mother and Mike were in the room with Joanne and the new baby.

Joanne was crying and was crouched over the baby in the bed in a kneeling position and she was choking the baby with her two hands.

She was shaking all over when she was doing this and the baby was screeching while she was choking it. No-one tried to stop her from doing this to the baby.

Joanne asked me to go down to the kitchen to get the carving knife from the drawer in the cabinet. I got the knife for her and I handed her the knife.

Joanne then stabbed the baby with the point of the carving knife in the chest about six or seven times. She was in a temper when she was stabbing the baby.

I have been shown a carving knife 'Prestige' make by Detective Garda Smith and I now identify the knife as being the knife that I handed to my sister Joanne when she stabbed the baby in the bedroom on Friday morning 13 April 1984 at approximately 2.45 am.

My mother, my brother Mike and my Aunt Bridie and myself were present in the room when Joanne was stabbing the baby with the carving knife.

The baby died from the choking and the stabbing and it was dead when my mother and I left the room to go up to our other house, which is about 50 yards away from my house, to call my brother Ned who is sleeping there.

It was 3 am when we went to call Ned. It was dark and I was using a flash lamp to give us light on the way up.

We knocked up Ned and I told Ned to come down, Joanne had a baby and the baby was dead. Ned hopped out of bed and came down to our house after us. He went to Joanne's room and he saw the dead baby with stab wounds on Joanne's bed.

Joanne was in the kitchen when Ned came to the house.

After Ned had seen the baby he was very upset.

He said 'Why did you kill the baby?'

We were all upset at that stage and we didn't know what to do. We thought we might bury it on the farm. Mike said 'Will we bury it back the field?' but Mom and

Bridie were against that. So then we decided we will have to dump it somewhere.

Mike went to the back kitchen to get a turf bag and I went to a drawer under the television and got a white plastic bag with two handles, like the ordinary shopping bag you would get in supermarkets.

I held the white plastic bag and Ned put the dead baby into it. We done this in the bedroom and then Ned put the white plastic bag containing the baby into a turf bag which Mike had got in the back kitchen.

I have been shown a bag by Detective Garda Smith and I believe that it was a bag of similar colour and material as the bag in which the white plastic bag containing the baby was put into.

The bag containing the baby was then brought out to the back kitchen by Ned, and Mike tied the bag with a piece of twine. Ned then took out the bag and put it into the boot of our car.

Ned, Mike and I left our house at about 3.50 am in our car. We drove through Tralee, on through Dingle town for about six miles, and we stopped at a place where the road runs beside the sea, and Ned, who was driving, got out and opened the boot of the car containing the baby and threw it into the sea.

It was about 5.30 am on Friday 13 April 1984 when Ned threw the bag into the sea. You could see the water from the road where we were parked and when the bag was thrown in, it sank, and re-surfaced and floated on the water.

We arrived back home at 7 am.

Ned drove the car that morning when we were disposing of the baby. I was in the front passenger seat, and Mike was sitting in the back seat.

We told my mother, Joanne and Bridie that we had thrown the baby into the sea back around Dingle.

Joanne Hayes said to Bridie Fuller:

O my God what did I do it for. I don't know what I got ye into at all. I don't know why I did it. Tell them I killed the baby. I don't want to see anyone, just put me into jail.

I made a statement telling them all about it and what happened. I did it myself and I don't want to blame anyone else. I told all the truth in the statement, oh I did, I did. I want to see no-one, just leave me alone.

You were in the room Bridie, I told them.

It was sometime in the night.

I was talking to Liam Moloney and I told him the truth.

Bridie Fuller said:

I am telling you the truth about what happened to my niece Joanne, the night her last baby was born in April of this year. I think the baby was born on the night of Tuesday 7 April or early the Wednesday morning.

I went to bed that evening early as I usually wake at about twelve or so. I must have been awake about one and Michael was up also.

I went down to Joanne's room and she was getting in and out of bed. I suspected that she was after going into labour.

I sent Michael up to the cottage where my sister Mary and her daughter Kathleen and son Ned were living. Kathleen and Mary come down to our house and I told them that Joanne was in labour.

Someone else went for Ned, I'm scattered about that, I think it was Michael.

It was now about half-past two and Joanne was at an advanced stage. We went up to see her and I helped break her waters. The baby was then born and I did the best I could to help her, it was a baby boy.

I saw it move and it was bubbling with mucus.

I was not in the room when the baby cried.

I think I made tea in the kitchen.

After this I don't know what happened but I remember it was light before I got back to bed.

Joanne got up late and I don't know what happened the baby.

She told me tonight that she had killed the baby the night it was born, and I'm so bothered by it all that I can't say any more.

III

There had been discrepancies and contradictions in their statements. Joanne had said that no one was present when she stabbed the baby. Aunt Bridie said she didn't know about the baby's stabbing or death, but Kathleen and Mike said she was present with them at the killing. Their mother had not mentioned stabbing at all. Ned and Mike claimed to have driven alone to the sea, while Kathleen said she was also in the car.

The police, however, were used to discrepancies. Had there been perfect accord between the statements, it would have looked suspicious, Superintendent Courtney said.

There was one outstanding discrepancy. The day after Joanne Hayes confessed to the murder of the baby found at Cahirciveen, her own baby was found on the farm.

When the midnight court had finished, and just before she was led away to the cell, Joanne spoke to Kathleen. It was the first time they had seen each other since being brought in by the police. Joanne told Kathleen that she had had a baby and that it was hidden on the farm. She told her sister where to find it.

Kathleen, Ned, Mike and Bridie were driven home by the guards, arriving there around one-thirty, and they sat up with Mary Hayes until 4 am recounting their experiences. The family did not treat Joanne's claim of burial of a baby on the farm seriously enough to take a torch and go out and look for it.

It was not until they had slept, milked the cows and breakfasted that Kathleen led her brothers, at 9.30 am, to the place indicated by Joanne. They found nothing and went on into Tralee to attend a formal court hearing. Joanne was remanded to Limerick prison and the rest were given bail.

Just before Joanne was taken away, and while she was talking to her solicitor Patrick Mann in a private room,

Kathleen came rushing in to say that she couldn't find the baby. Her head had been too muddled to take in the information in the police station. Joanne repeated it.

That afternoon Kathleen, Ned and Mike went searching again. Mike found the bag in a water hole almost at once. They didn't touch it or open it. 'Fingerprints,' said Kathleen. Ned drove her into Tralee, where she spoke with Patrick Mann and he told her to contact Guard Liam Moloney in Abbeydorney about the find.

Kathleen went to see him. He was about to have his dinner and he was sceptical. He didn't want to get into trouble with a wild goose chase, he said, and he asked her to sign a declaration of responsibility on the back of an envelope. She couldn't be in any more trouble than she was, she said, and she signed his envelope. He rang Tralee station and a posse of guards arrived on the farm to accompany Kathleen to the water hole. They tore open the bag and found inside the dead baby to which Joanne had given birth on the night of 12/13 April.

Apart from some discoloration round the neck – 'I delivered the baby myself with my own hands', Joanne had said – her son was unmarked.

Joanne Hayes was in the mental hospital in Limerick when news came through that evening that her baby had been found on the farm. She had been transferred to the hospital within hours of being lodged in jail, after psychiatrist John Fennelly confirmed the fears which the prison governor had expressed for her mental stability.

She was watching the tea-time news on television and the final wrap-up, accompanied by subtitles for the hard of hearing, spelt out what she had spelt out to disbelieving police officers. 'Now they'll believe I'm not the mother of the Cahirciveen baby,' she said, and she lay down on the floor before the television set and went into a deep sleep.

The nurses let her lie there, unwilling to disturb the most precious slumber of all, that which is achieved without drugs.

As darkness fell they carried her to her bed, choosing not to remove her clothes lest they disturb her peace. She did not awaken until ten-thirty the following morning.

When she did, she tried repeatedly to relive the moments of her son's birth and death, crouching and showing how she had pulled him from her womb, wondering aloud if her hands on his throat had killed him, or had she put her hand over his mouth.

Those who cared for her did not put questions to her. Their job was to listen, soothe and let be, until shock had passed. There would be time enough for questions. There had been many mothers in shock in that hospital.

In the same ward as Joanne was the woman who had been found five days after childbirth dangling her infant by its feet. There had been the woman who demonstrated, again and again, how she sat on the toilet bowl to relieve pressured kidneys and got up to find that she had delivered herself of a baby. The baby lay dead in the bowl, its skull smashed on the porcelain. A woman would come and stay in the hospital for months before admitting the nightmare of birth through an incestuous relationship with her father, who had taken her to his newly widowed bed when she was twelve.

To such women, who are admitted weekly to that one hospital, is denied what the French writer Colette calls 'the beatitude of pregnant females . . . my feeling of pride, of banal magnificence as I ripened my fruit . . . This purring contentment, this euphoria – how give a name either scientific or familiar to this state of preservation – must certainly have penetrated me, since I have not forgotten it and am recalling it now, when life can never again bring me plenitude.'

In the Limerick hospital Joanne Hayes was promised that she would be released in time to go home for the first birthday, on 19 May, of her beloved daughter Yvonne.

On the night her baby was found, however, 2 May, Superintendent Courtney had another conference with all the police who had been involved in the investigation. They all agreed that Joanne Hayes had had twins. 'By a strange twist of fate the body of the first-born was not discovered until after the charge', Detective P.J. Browne wrote in the police report which was forwarded to the Director of Public Prosecutions (DPP). The lengthy report outlined the case against Joanne Hayes which the police proposed to bring into court. On the strength of this document they hoped to successfully prosecute her with the murder of the Cahirciveen baby. 'This report is based solely on fact', appended Superintendent Courtney. 'It does not enter the realms of speculation.'

The report admitted to one central difficulty regarding forensic evidence on blood groups. Joanne Hayes, Jeremiah Locke and their dead son, found on the farm at Abbeydorney, all belonged to blood-group O. The Cahirciveen baby was blood-group A. One of its parents would have to be blood-group A. The guards proposed that Joanne Hayes had had twins by two different men, one of whom was blood-group A. Both men had had sexual intercourse with her during a forty-eight-hour period. She had become pregnant by both.

This phenomenon, known as superfecundation, is so rare that it is a footnote in rarefied medical journals. The police report wished it to be taken into factual consideration. It was possible, wrote P.J. Browne, that Joanne Hayes was the mother of the Cahirciveen baby.

He added a note of caution: 'The converse probability that she is not is more likely.'

Given the probability that she was not the mother of the Cahirciveen baby, the police put forward another theory. The baby which she had stabbed, and which her brother had thrown into the sea, had simply never been found. By a strange twist of fate, the police argued, two stabbed baby boys had been thrown into the waters off Slea Head on the same night, one of which had been found, identity of mother unknown, the other of which was still missing, its mother identified as Joanne Hayes.

The report cited a precedent for laying a charge of murder where the victim was missing: in a special non-jury court in Northern Ireland some IRA men had been convicted of murdering British army captain, Robert Nairac, though his body was never recovered.

There was another difficulty. Irish tidal waters flow clockwise round the island, and the baby found at Cahirciveen would have had to float eleven miles in an anti-clockwise direction, in twenty-four hours, if it had been thrown off Slea Head.

Doubt also surrounded the evidence connecting the Hayeses directly with the Cahirciveen baby. Ned had identified an 0-7-30 fertiliser bag as the shroud of the baby he threw into the sea off Slea Head. The police forensic scientist Louise McKenna had established that the 0-7-30 bag found near the Cahirciveen baby bore no signs whatever of contact with a baby, bleeding or otherwise. Nor had the brown plastic bag found within it. Nor the clear plastic bag found within that. The police subsequently lost all three bags.

Dr McKenna also found that the mattress on which Joanne Hayes slept bore no traces of human blood. The sheet from her bed yielded minute samples which were identified as the blood of insects. The paint flakes taken from the walls and floor of her bedroom showed no trace whatever of blood. One nightdress, the bottom half of which was heavily stained with human blood, was strewn with stalks of hay. Another nightdress was less heavily stained, and bore no trace of hay. Her panties were stained with blood.

Before forwarding his report to the Director of Public Prosecutions, Superintendent Courtney discussed it with the Kerry state solicitor, Donal Browne. The solicitor told him to 'scrub' the entire case 'fast'.

John Courtney then speculated about the possibility of charging Joanne Hayes with the murder of the baby found on the farm. The solicitor pointed out the difficulty of proving that that baby had been born alive, never mind prove that it had been killed. Superintendent Courtney quoted the provisional verdict given by the state pathologist, Dr Harbison, at the post-mortem, which an unusual number of guards had attended. He liked his men to learn, Courtney explained. One of them, Gerry O'Carroll, had even been able to help the pathologist. When Dr Harbison expressed puzzlement at the bruise on the baby's neck, Detective O'Carroll had read out Joanne's statement that she had delivered the baby herself.

The pathologist had then declared, 'Gentlemen, we have a separate existence.'

Dr Harbison had later revised this speculation to say in a written report that an examination of the baby's unexpanded lungs led him to doubt whether the baby had ever come breathing out of the womb at all, but the police ploughed on regardless of him and the state solicitor.

They forwarded their complete report to the Director of Public Prosecutions. The DPP read it and wrote a letter to the Kerry state solicitor in September. The letter instructed Donal Browne to withdraw the charges in 'this amazing case' at the first opportunity.

IV

On 10 October 1984 the Hayes family learned in court that the case was now dropped. This came as complete news to them and to their solicitor. The charges had been kept hanging over them until the last possible minute. Two journalists, Don Buckley and Joe Joyce, had known for weeks beforehand that the police had been ordered to drop the case.

The two journalists had revealed, in the mid-Seventies, the existence of a police 'heavy gang' which specialised in extorting confessions by force. Though no policemen had ever been sacked as a result of the revelations, the existence of the heavy gang was accepted by the government and opposition parties of the day and a retired judge had been instructed to draw up guidelines for proper police procedure. His recommendations were never implemented.

Now the two journalists had been alerted to the possibility of strange happenings in County Kerry involving dead babies and confessions. Their report appeared two days after the police withdrew the case.

The public anger which followed was fuelled by another scandal that had boiled up during the summer. In Shercock garda station in County Cavan, a man had died of injuries inflicted in police custody. There had been only four policemen in the station. They testified against each other in court. The state failed to obtain a conviction.

The Hayeses now alleged extortion of confessions by force and psychological terror.

The police held an immediate internal inquiry into the affair. The Hayes family said they had had enough of police interviews and sent in written statements via their solicitor, who demanded immunity from any possible charges of concealment of birth in connection with Joanne's dead son. Bridie Fuller, now hospitalised with a stroke, was unable to say or write anything.

Joanne claimed she had asked repeatedly, about once every half-hour, in the course of her interview with the police on 1 May that she be taken out to the farm to show where her baby was hidden. He was worried that the sight of a dead child would drive her mad, said Superintendent Courtney. Just when he had decided to bring her out anyway, her mother's incriminating statement had come in from the farm and he changed his mind. Besides, said one detective, a suspect had once confided that he would have thrown himself off the cliff had they brought him to the scene of the crime. Similar fear existed in this case about a possible suicide attempt should the police bring Joanne Hayes out to her lowland home.

They had told her, said Joanne Hayes, that Yvonne would

be put in an orphanage, her mother jailed and the farm sold if she did not confess. She had felt nauseous and Detective P.J. Browne had spread a newspaper on the floor, telling her to vomit onto it. He had then put her 'sitting up on his lap' while Detective O'Carroll took down her statement.

She had wept 'bitter tears' onto his shoulder, said Detective Browne. His colleague had put a fatherly arm around her, confirmed Detective O'Carroll.

Detective O'Carroll had told her that infanticide was no longer treated as murder and a suspended sentence would result, she alleged. He had told her that, he confirmed.

There was no question of a newspaper on the floor, said Detective Browne. If ever he found himself helping police with enquiries he would wish to be treated as Joanne Hayes had been treated that day.

Superintendent Courtney had poked his finger into her shoulder and really frightened her, she said. He had a habit of pointing his finger at people, said the superintendent, nothing more.

The police, said Ned, had told him to get down on his knees and make an act of contrition. He resented scurrilous allegations about religion, said Detective Dillon. He could not remember whether it was Detective Dillon or Detective O'Mahony who had upended him on the floor and tried to grab his testicles, said Ned. It's not the sort of assault you're likely to make a mistake about, the detectives pointed out.

One of the policemen, said Mike, had put an arm round him and thrown mock punches at his stomach while walking him round the room. They didn't hurt, but there's nothing friendly about a policeman's arm around you as you walk round a room in a police station. He was frightened, he said. The policemen denied it. They told him he'd never milk a cow again, he said. It was denied.

One of the guards, said Kathleen, had brought a moveable phone into the room in Abbeydorney station, plugged it in, taken calls and said that every call he was getting proved how many lies she was telling.

The guards proved that there is no moveable phone in Abbeydorney station.

She had been slapped across the back of the head, said Kathleen, had complained 'Oh, my head,' and been told 'Never mind your old head.' It was denied. She had been threatened with incarceration in Killarney mental home, said Kathleen. It was denied. She had been asked if she had voted pro-life in the amendment, had said yes, and had been jeered that the neighbours would think her evil now. It was denied. Aspersions had been cast on her mother's appearance: 'Look at the cut of her, thrown into a corner,' she said they had said. It was denied.

She had been compared, said Mary Hayes, to an old tinker going the roads. It was denied. She had been told what to say and had said it, she charged. It was denied. Liam Moloney had asked her if she had confessed to the priest what she was confessing to the police, she said. He agreed that he had.

The family had been under virtual arrest, they said. Their presence in the police station was purely voluntary and they were free to leave any time they wished, came the reply.

How, asked those in charge of the internal police inquiry, had statements been obtained to charges that couldn't be sustained? Some of the guards, acting under the instructions of legal advisers, refused to answer some of the questions. The inquiry aborted.

10. Tribunal

The minister for justice responded to the public clamour with a tribunal of inquiry into the Kerry babies affair. It was set up in a hurry, and it was thought that it would finish quickly. The tribunal met on 28 December and agreed to sit in Tralee from 7 January for an estimated three weeks. The costs of legal representation were not guaranteed either to the police or to the Hayes family.

Top legal brains in the country faded away like snow off a ditch. Between them, the twenty-five guards and three superintendents mustered enough money to pay fees for a little while and lawyers who had scarcely been heard of were found for them.

The Hayes family, without a single wage-earner between the six of them, acquired a lawyer whose previous experience had been almost entirely confined to civil work in the employment appeals tribunal. He had taken sick and had returned to court only months before and was, unlike experienced senior counsel, available for work at short notice. He was hired with no guarantee of pay only two days before the tribunal opened. The Hayes family solicitor undertook to pay his hotel expenses while in Tralee.

The tribunal judge, Kevin Lynch, with one year's experience on the bench, had made his name as a barrister in matters of commercial and civil litigation. None of the fifteen legal men, comprising judge, senior and junior barristers and solicitors, had ever witnessed childbirth. 'Is it possible,' the judge was to ask 'for a woman to give birth standing up?'

Women have given birth underwater, in aeroplanes, in comas, lying unnaturally flat on their backs in hospital beds, and even after death, but this man wondered if they could do it standing up. Only one had even a glancing experience of matters connected with the female reproductive system. Martin Kennedy, senior counsel for the three superintendents, had taken part in the pro-life campaign, canvassing in the plush seaside suburb of Dalkey near Dublin. While Jeremiah Locke was engaged in serial impregnation of two women, Mr Kennedy had been assuring voters, on behalf of a Fianna Fáil party that opposed contraception for single people, that the baby in a woman's womb needed constitutional protection.

The primary aim and function of the tribunal was to find out how the police had conducted themselves in Tralee garda station on 1 May and afterwards, to inquire 'into the circumstances of the preferment and withdrawal of charges'. It might have been that the police procedure was at all times correct and their criminal methodology beyond criticism, and that they had had no choice but to proceed with charges, given the information in their possession; it might have been the complete opposite. It was the tribunal's job to find out.

The tribunal's second function was to inquire into 'the allegations made by the Hayes family' against the police.

The tribunal's third function was to inquire into 'any relevant matters'.

Justice Lynch interpreted these terms of reference on three occasions during the inquiry. The government, he said, 'have asked me to investigate, as best I can, the birth of . . . Miss Joanne Hayes's baby in Abbeydorney'. Then he said of that birth: 'It is not really the exercise I am engaged on here at all . . . it doesn't matter a thrawneen whether the baby was born inside or outside, IF THERE WAS ONLY ONE BABY.' Then he said that the 'only subsisting allegations' which the tribunal had to investigate were those made by the Hayes family.

The judge had set his mind on finding out if Joanne Hayes

had had twins, if she had given birth inside or outside the house should there be only one baby, and whether the Hayes family were telling the truth about the police.

Since no charges had ever been preferred against the Hayes family in respect of the baby found at Abbeydorney, the death of that infant might properly have been regarded as a private family tragedy, as had been the case with Anne Lovett.

However, the third term of reference, 'any relevant matters', allowed the tribunal to conduct, in effect, the trial that was never 'meant to be and the police lawyers took the opportunity that had originally been denied them to present what the Director of Public Prosecutions had called 'this amazing case'.

A key element of the police case was the suggestion of 'superfecundation'. On the opening day of the tribunal Mr Michael Moriarty, senior counsel of the legal team appointed to help the judge, emphasised that expert opinion considered this to be 'an extremely rare and unlikely event'.

Five months were to pass before that expert should finally arrive to give his opinion. During those months the men of the tribunal and the police aired their own opinions on whether the woman brought before them could have achieved the unlikely. Joanne Hayes became the real-life model of the bio-logical trial-and-error experiments conducted by five all-male teams of lawyers, three per team, representing the judge, the Director of Public Prosecutions, the superintendents of police, the guards and the Hayeses. The members of her family were called to provide the circumstantial detail for this or that experiment.

First, though, the tribunal set the stage by calling in her friends, her employers and Jeremiah Locke.

11. Tom Flynn

The judge sat up on his dais, the legal men ranged themselves below him, and the women friends of Joanne Hayes were brought forward one by one to the anvil of the witness box and forced under oath to deny her. It was quite simply done. Had they known, the question was put to Martina Rohan, Aileen Enright, Mary O'Riordan, Peggy Houlihan and Mary Shanahan, that she was pregnant?

They had.

Had she lied to them upon her release from hospital, claiming she had had a miscarriage?

She had.

Mary O'Riordan tried to soften the blow. Asked by Mr Anthony Kennedy, counsel for the guards, if she was disappointed that Joanne had misled her, she replied 'No, she went through very hard times.'

Dermot McCarthy, senior counsel for the Hayeses, had Mary O'Riordan recalled later because, he said, information which had just come to him indicated that a wrong impression had been given that Joanne had lied to Mary O'Riordan.

Mr McCarthy then asked his witness: 'Did she explicitly tell you that she had lost the baby in hospital?'

Ms O'Riordan had to say 'Yes.'

It was not Mr McCarthy's finest hour, though subsequent events were to show that it was not his worst.

Peggy Houlihan was asked by Martin Kennedy to account for her temerity in having a drink after work with Jeremiah Locke. He observed that she, a married woman, was 'out drinking with a married man. I see.' Moreover, he declaimed, this married man was known to indulge in affairs. Mr Kennedy's indignation mounted as he pursued the implications of this. 'Is your husband alive? What did your husband think about that?' He asked her how her husband was supposed to fetch his own tea, while she was in the pub.

All the women were asked if they knew a certain Tom Flynn. They didn't. His name had been found, written in biro, on the mattress on which Joanne Hayes slept. He was, insisted Martin Kennedy, Joanne's lover before she met Jeremiah Locke. As his name rang and recurred through the proceedings, Tom Flynn acquired the notoreity of the wild colonial boy, Jack Dougan from nearby Castlemaine, who had emigrated to Australia in the previous century, where he robbed the rich to help the poor, according to the ballad. Where, however, was Tom Flynn? Mr Kennedy, acting under instructions from Superintendent John Courtney, and in hot pursuit of the theory of superfecundation, wanted to know.

The people of Tralee knew, but they didn't enlighten him. They chose instead to ridicule a tribunal that appeared to them to be increasingly ridiculous, by sporting T-shirts that had been hurriedly printed by a local entrepreneur. 'I'm Tom Flynn' the T-shirts proclaimed.

Weeks were to pass before the tribunal established that Tom Flynn used to work in a shop selling mattresses, that he had emigrated to America in 1969 when Joanne Hayes was a ten-year-old, and that he had never returned home.

Ridicule changed to shock when the men who did know Joanne Hayes came forward to testify.

12. Jeremiah Locke

Liam Bohan, manager of the sports complex, read out to the court a letter that Joanne had written to him from the mental home to which she had been transferred after a night in prison. It was the first of many private documents concerning her that the world was invited to hear. As he read it out, Joanne Hayes left the court in tears.

Dear Liam,

I don't know how to start off this letter. I am so sorry for causing such an embarrassment to all of you working with me. Please forgive me. I want to thank you for all the help you gave me since you came to the complex. You were new there when I first got pregnant, but still you never said anything to me.

Don't ask me why I did what I did because I don't know or I will never know. I am so ashamed for what I did and most of all I am sorry for getting everyone I love involved. It must be all the pressure building up that made me do it. I really don't know. When the gardai took me down to the station on Tuesday they were delighted because, according to them, they had the murderer for the baby in Cahirciveen.

I had to make a false statement because they told me that if I didn't my mother would be jailed and Yvonne would be put into an orphanage. I am now in a hospital for mental cases. Am I mental, Liam? I can't think straight anymore. I don't mind being punished for what I did, but I didn't want to be punished for the baby in Cahirciveen.

> Mr Mann came to see me today. He told me Jer is
> having a pretty rough time around the town. Please Liam
> don't be too hard on him. I have ruined his life also. I
> really love him.
>
> You are a real nice person and thanks for everything
> you did for me. Say a prayer for me.
>
> Love, Joanne

In the event, Jeremiah Locke's employers were not at all
hard on him and he was transferred discreetly to another VEC
workplace. Joanne Hayes had no such luck. Mr Bohan and Mr
Falvey convened a meeting of the management board of the
sports complex the night she was arrested and decided to go
ahead on 13 May with the competition for her redefined clerical job. Although her baby was then found and bail for her
obtained, it was not found possible to change the date of the
examination and it went ahead twenty-four hours after she was
released from the mental home from which she had written to
Liam Bohan. She was unfit to attend.

On the day after Mr Bohan revealed to the tribunal that
she thought him a 'real nice person', Jeremiah Locke took the
stand to tell what Joanne Hayes thought of him.

He introduced himself as a married man with two children. Although he has, in fact, three children, the tribunal
accepted his sworn word on the matter. His third child is
Yvonne Hayes. After Joanne gave birth, he went to see the
mother and daughter in hospital. He had seen Yvonne only
once since that day in 1983. He had been away on holidays
when Joanne went into hospital a second time, in April 1984.
He heard about that in a pub. He understood that Joanne had
miscarried this one of his children but she congratulated him,
he said, on the birth of a daughter that very same month to his
wife and himself.

He knew, he said, that Joanne loved him very much. Asked
if he loved her he said, 'I did, I suppose, yes, I did love her . . .
it depends on what you mean by love. I was a married man.'

He and Martin Kennedy then had a detailed discussion on how, where and when he had had 'sexual intercourse' with Joanne Hayes. Was it in a car, on the side of the road, or at home when his wife was not there, Mr Kennedy wanted to know. 'We had sex together' in his Mini car said Mr Locke, when he used to drive her home. Mr Kennedy produced an Ordnance Survey map and asked him to pinpoint the back lane in which intimacy had occurred.

At this point Justice Lynch interrupted the discussion between the two men and asked how it was relevant to the tribunal. Mr Kennedy answered: 'If I can show that Joanne Hayes had a previous sexual history . . . and that during her relationship she was also having sex with others; and if one of these others had blood-group A, then it will be . . . not only possible but probable that twins born of that union could have had blood-group A in one, and O in the other'.

On that basis, said Mr Lynch, cross-examination could continue. On that basis, and because the expert on super-fecundation was not called for another sixteen weeks, licence was given to the men to speculate virtually every day on the sexuality of Joanne Hayes. The daily coupling of her name with the term 'sexual intercourse' allowed her character to pass into ferocious and lurid legend. She became a snigger in filthy mouths.

In the meantime a reprieved Mr Martin Kennedy wanted to know, on behalf of the three police superintendents, if Jeremiah Locke had intercourse with Joanne Hayes on every occasion that he drove her home. No, said Mr Locke. How exactly did it start, Mr Kennedy was curious and wanted to know – did the woman suggest it or the man?

'It takes two,' said the much younger Mr Locke.

Mr Anthony Kennedy wanted to know if they had used contraception. They hadn't. He wanted to know if Joanne Hayes was a virgin when Jeremiah Locke met her. She wasn't. Was it a problem that his wife was pregnant at the same time?

It wasn't. Would Mr Locke agree with Mr Kennedy that Joanne Hayes saw Yvonne as a compromise, since she couldn't have him permanently with her? He would.

After Joanne had confronted him at the Christmas party about the fact that both she and his wife were pregnant by him, he used to meet her still but 'it was nothing like before', he explained to Mr Moriarty. In any case, as he had previously told Anthony Kennedy, 'I had no intention of breaking with my wife.'

Of his day in the police station on 1 May, when the guards thanked him for helping with their enquiries and then released him without charge, he had no complaints, except to say that they 'spoke hard' with him.

A priest went on national radio to protest at the nature of the questions being put to Jeremiah Locke. Father Paul Byrne, secretary of the Conference of Major Religious Superiors, objected to lawyers asking if Mr Locke was in love with his wife and whether he used contraceptives.

No priest ever publicly objected to the questions put to Joanne Hayes, who was brought before the tribunal the following week.

13. Scream Quietly

After hearing them all, the judge declared that this was 'a very odd family'. The Hayeses had been brought into the tribunal one by one, while the rest remained outside, and asked questions about each other. Sometimes their answers tallied, sometimes they did not.

Such procedure is the stuff of psychological textbooks or successful television entertainments: while Kevin waits offstage, Ursula recounts from memory an intimate event that involved her and him; while Ursula waits offstage, Kevin recalls the same incident; the audience laughs its leg off at the wildly contradictory detail, the differing emphasis on what was important.

Songs have been written about such things. You wore blue, no it was red, I was on time, no you were late, ah yes, I remember it well.

There are times when things are not so funny, when a family chooses or is compelled by fear to ignore what is happening in its midst. A daughter comes home on holiday without her husband. She stays one week, two, then three, growing more and more miserable. She says nothing. The doctor is called. She goes into the mental home. 'My husband was sick and I got the treatment,' she later says of the ending of a marriage which she could not handle, her family could not face and her husband stayed away from.

Fifteen-year-old Anne Lovett was visibly pregnant in the small village of Granard, County Longford, and her teachers and neighbours assumed the family were coping. Her father was often seen fetching her home from the pool hall. She died in childbirth, in the open air, alone. 'Even had I noticed she was pregnant,' said the parish priest, 'I could hardly just come out and say "You're pregnant."' The state called it a family tragedy. Six weeks later her fourteen-year-old sister killed herself. That was a family tragedy, too. The state couldn't face it. As long as they die alone, and no one else is involved . . .

In Derry a woman came knocking on the doors of her neighbours to announce that her daughter was six months pregnant. The neighbours, bound to tactful silence until the woman should speak, were freed to offer help and commiseration. All over the world, people are constrained from mentioning the noises that come from next door. *Scream Quietly or the Neighbours Will Hear* is the title of a book about wife-battering. The right word, at the wrong time, is construed as interference.

A son leaves his home town, his wife and his children, in search of work. He comes home once a year and the family doesn't ask what he's doing over there, not his wife, not his parents, not his friends. Twenty years he's been away, but no one wants to know the details. He lives with a man. Officially he's got a wife and children over here. Jesus help us all should he die and there's a competing crowd around the grave. Maybe he'll get buried over there and we'll all be too old to travel or care.

A pregnant unmarried woman announces that she has got a job in England, and goes to live in secret in a convent somewhere in Ireland. CURA, the confidential Catholic service for such women, has booked her into the convent and also arranged a postal address in England. The woman's letters home, and the family's letters to her, are routed through the English address. The government praises the work of CURA.

These things are done in the name of love. It depends what you mean by love. 'If your wife knew,' Martin Kennedy asked the psychologist Brian McCaffrey, 'that you have decided in

The Hayes family at home: Mary, Kathleen, Joanne, Mike,
Ned with baby Yvonne and Bridie Fuller.

Pat Keegan/*Irish Press*

Left: Joanne Hayes.
Above: Jeremiah Locke.

John Courtney.

Ban Gharda Ursula O'Regan and
Guard Liam Moloney.

Above:
Kathleen and Joanne with friends Martina Rohan and Mary Riordan.

MEN

Right:
The church in Abbeydorney where the Hayes family worship. The seating at the back is reserved for men.

Sr Mechtilde, assistant matron, Tralee General Hospital.

The tribunal at work: lawyers study the site where the
second baby was found.

Dermot McCarthy.

Martin Kennedy.

Tribunal judge,
Kevin Lynch.

Jerry Kennelly

Bridie Fuller's first appearance before the tribunal, being wheeled in by Sr Brenda Mary.

Louise McKenna, '*the blood was A*'.

Protest

Protest

Protest (*left and right*): 'The Judge described the women as *raucous, ignorant urban dwellers* and he threatened jail sentence on anyone who, in his opinion, insulted or obstructed the tribunal.

'He personally would impose the sentence, up to a maximum of two years, and he personally would decide if the person who committed contempt and subsequently sought release from jail was sincerely and sufficiently apologetic, and he would be in no personal hurry to hear apologies, since he was a busy man.'

Joanne with Yvonne opening letters of support, in a room provided, at the tribunal (January 1985).

Above: Early days: Bridie Fuller, Yvonne, Mary Hayes and a neighbour.

Below: Martina Rohan, Mary O'Riordan, Joanne Hayes.

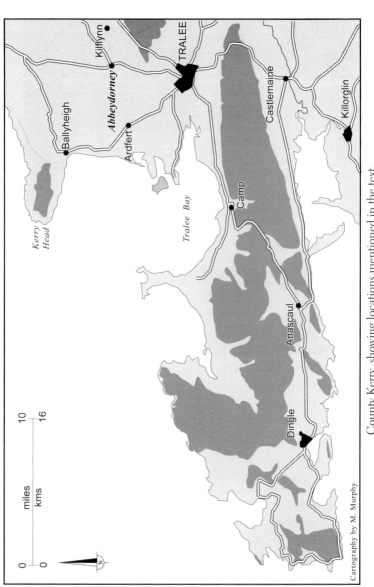

County Kerry, showing locations mentioned in the text.

Cartography by M. Murphy

the interests of your family to purchase a new house, and you know that she knows, though you haven't spoken to her – is it important that you have not exchanged confidences?'

'I wouldn't lay that much emphasis on it,' came the reply.

For two weeks before the guards arrived, said the judge, the whole family knew about the birth and sat around behaving normally. Kathleen had just told him that she 'presumed' and 'supposed' that the others knew what she strongly suspected, in fact was sure of – that Joanne had had a baby.

Kathleen never discussed her suspicious certainty with Joanne. 'I was waiting for her to bring it up,' was how she described the sleepless night the two sisters had spent together in the room after Joanne came in from the field. Joanne lay on the bed, Kathleen lay on the mattress on the floor, Yvonne lay in her cot, and not a word was said.

And if Joanne had never brought it up, she was asked?

'I would have remained silent about it for ever.'

Sister Aquinas described to the tribunal how the family members communicated with each other. They seldom discussed anything. It was not that they refused to speak, but 'to me discussion is different. It is different to general conversation.'

A thing would happen, and be mentioned and, if there was nothing to be done, or the thing was very painful, they moved on to other matters. Abbeydorney was as far removed from Californian consciousness-raising as it was possible to be.

There was, in any case, a delicate and natural hierarchy within the family, unspoken but observed, established by custom, practice and predilection.

Aquinas and Joan Fuller were, at the end of the day, only the aunts. Mary Hayes might be the titular head, as mother, but Joanne was of age, well over age, when their troubles began, twenty-two at the start, twenty-four by the time she arrived in the police station. Mike and Ned led lives that were not home-centred, Mike concentrating on his cows, Ned leading a life virtually apart in the second dwelling up the road.

'I wouldn't ask Ned. I would ask Kathleen or the mother,' is how Aunt Joan explained to the tribunal she would broach family matters. She wouldn't ask Joanne. 'I never asked her those questions about her private life, especially in things as sad as that.' Nor did she probe into the sad things. When Kathleen gave her sad, sparse information, 'I took it as she gave it to me. I left it at that.'

The brothers presumed Kathleen would tell them anything they ought to know and didn't go looking for information. They relied on her to do what was necessary in any given situation. Everybody relied on Kathleen, who virtually ran the home, while her sister worked in the sports complex, her mother's health declined with years and her Aunt Bridie withdrew from reality. On the day the police called, it was Kathleen who saw to the dinner and the changing of Yvonne's nappy; when the dead baby was found, it was Kathleen who went in to tell Patrick Mann, while Ned waited outside in the car; it was Kathleen who went in to tell Guard Liam Moloney, while Ned waited outside in the car; it was Kathleen who took the police to the pool, while Ned went up the road to his cottage and Mike milked the cows.

It was Kathleen who stayed up until Joanne came in from the field that night, Kathleen who went to fetch help for her a day later, Kathleen whom Joanne told about the location of the baby. Kathleen had a lot to carry within the family. Sometimes, though, the others got involved in decision-making. They did so, as Aquinas pointed out, with the minimum of discussion. That's the way they were.

For instance, Aquinas had a fairly good idea that Joanne was pregnant with Yvonne, but 'I kept my suspicions to myself. I was waiting for them at home to tell me.' She had been on a visit to the farm and, as she stood out on the road waiting for a lift back to the convent, Joanne came home from work, and Aquinas felt sure from the look of her that her niece was expecting. That was in March 1983.

In April, the family saw Aquinas coming up the path and 'Bridie came and met me outside the door. She said "We are in great trouble here. Joanne is pregnant and there won't be a marriage because he is a married man."'

She went inside and found Mary Hayes and Kathleen crying. 'They knew that I knew, and I knew that they knew.' Few words were said. 'There was no great discussion, because when the man was married there wasn't much that could be done.' Adoption was mentioned, but they felt that 'Joanne would have the last word'. Joanne was out late that night. In the morning Aquinas went to see her in the bedroom. 'I said to her that they had told me about her condition and she cried and was upset.' The aunt held her niece in her arms and nothing more was said. Days later Sister Aquinas wrote to Joanne recommending adoption, but Joanne refused and that was that.

Aunt Joan had to be told. She came down for Easter and Mary Hayes, driven to the station by Ned, told her in the car on the way out to the farm. 'They told me he was a married man. That is the only objection I had to him. I did not say that to Joanne.'

Aunt Joan, like Aquinas, waited until she had returned to Newbridge before broaching the matter, in a letter, to her niece. She also recommended adoption. Receiving no reply, the aunt sent a second letter that painfully acknowledged her place in the family. 'I am not your mother. I hope you haven't taken offence. Let us carry on as we always have carried on.'

Yvonne was born in May. The family had not faced up to her arrival until the seventh month of pregnancy.

What happened the second time round, though, the tribunal wanted to know? One by one, out of each other's sight, in full sight of the public, they were made to account for their own and each other's attitude the second time round. One by one they said they had not noticed she was pregnant, except for Kathleen.

Kathleen, unable to deny the evidence of her own eyes, unable to discuss it with a family that did not mention it, unable to discuss it certainly with Joanne, who had met her query with an outright 'No', went finally to her cousin's house and said that which was difficult to say, that Joanne was pregnant again. The cousin said she had noticed. They watched *Hill Street Blues* together. Joanne was then in the eighth month of pregnancy, within twenty-four hours of premature birth.

The protestations of Mary Hayes, her sons Mike and Ned and Aunts Joan and Aquinas that they did not know were met with scorn and abuse and jeers. 'Didn't the dogs in the street know?' asked Kevin O'Higgins. 'Half the countryside knew,' declared Anthony Kennedy. It was a well-known fact among her co-workers at Christmas, the tribunal said.

All she had noticed at Christmas, said Aunt Joan, was that her sister Mary had emphysema and blood pressure, which the doctor said might necessitate hospitalisation. She would prove, she said, that she had not noticed in Christmas 1983 that Joanne was pregnant again by telling them about Christmas 1982, when Joanne was expecting Yvonne. That Christmas she had gone down home for her seasonal two-day holiday. Mary Hayes had given her a turkey, as she did every Christmas, to bring back to her employers, 'my priests'. Joan Fuller felt she was 'getting a bit beyond the stage of dragging turkeys up and down on trains', especially crowded ones, so Joanne was roped in to help. Joanne spent all her summer holidays up in the priests' house, and was welcome there, so she got on board the train with her aunt, 'came up with me with the turkey and the next thing I discovered the baby was born in May'.

The tribunal advanced reasons why the family members did not know, or admit to themselves, or discuss openly the fact that Joanne Hayes was pregnant once more. Addressing each other, or the judge, or the witnesses, the lawyers drew an imaginative portrait of pregnancy outside marriage and its effects on family and society in post-amendment Ireland.

Surely, Anthony Kennedy suggested, Kathleen was self-conscious about what the local community would think. The pregnancy was a reflection on her, a source of embarrassment and shame about what people would say to her when she went outside the house.

He invited Kathleen to agree with him that she faced a bleak and frustrating future, her hopes of getting married or getting a job destroyed should Joanne have a second 'illegitimate' child and she 'be stuck minding the two of them'. Kathleen, at thirty, was 'not getting any younger', Martin Kennedy offered.

The situation must have been, said Anthony Kennedy, 'an absolute scandal'. In a rural area like Abbeydorney, suggested Brian Curtin, the situation was worsened by the fact that the father of the second illegitimate child was the same married man. Here was a family with a nun in it and a priests' housekeeper. Highly respected, amplified Brendan Grogan, and 'suddenly Joanne is flaunting the fact that she was pregnant. She had no shame.' This would be a cause of resentment and coldness in the house.

That would eventually cause a breakdown in communication, speculated Brian Curtin. 'It would not be discussed as openly as the first pregnancy?' Nevertheless, the tribunal wanted the family to account for the time of the actual birth in the early hours of Friday morning 13 April.

14. Birth on the Farm

On Thursday 12 April 1984 Joanne Hayes had a scheduled day off work. So far she'd had a lousy month. After inviting her to take maternity leave, her employers had taken out an advertisement in the paper on 6 April announcing that her regraded job was open to public competition. The examination for the clerk-typist grade 2 position would pose no problems, since she had long ago got her secretarial certificate from college, but the advertisement said that applicants would have to do an interview as well.

The examination and interview were scheduled for the middle of May, just around the time her baby was due. The interview would be with John Falvey, chief education officer of the Vocational Education Committee. He had interviewed her before, about her relationship with Jeremiah Locke, and she had denied it.

Joanne Hayes spent her day off work getting in and out of bed, complaining of stomach pains. Mike spent that day with the cows, went to a neighbour's house in the evening, came home around eleven, held Yvonne while Kathleen fetched her nappy for a last change, and then Mike went to bed. He shared his room with his mother, who had been occupying the spare bed for some weeks now, stricken with a bout of heavy flu. It was easier for her to stay all the time in the farmhouse during her illness than to sleep overnight in the cottage and trek the daily hundred yards back to where the food and heat and people were.

Ned spent that Thursday putting new windows into the cottage. When he and the man who was helping him came down to the farmhouse for their midday meal, Joanne did not come to the table. She had a pain in her stomach, his mother told him.

That evening Ned went to a neighbour to finalise plans for the football match on Friday night, collected the jerseys for the team, called to a petrol pump and went for a pint in the Silver Dollar. He drove home, left the keys of the car in the farmhouse, said goodnight and went up to the cottage of which he was now sole occupant. Kathleen, too, had moved down to the farmhouse, to take care of her mother. Ned read part of *The Great Hunger* before going to sleep.

Kathleen spent that day running the farmhouse as usual. In the evening, while Joanne and her mother watched television, she went to a neighbour's house to get her hair done. When she came home towards midnight, she found Ned already gone to the cottage and her mother and Mike in the kitchen getting ready to retire. Aunt Bridie, true to her nocturnal habits, was asleep in her room. She was not due to get up until the others had left the kitchen. Joanne, too, was in bed in her own room and Yvonne was in the cot beside her. Kathleen went to see them. Joanne asked Kathleen to change Yvonne's nappy.

Kathleen remembers asking Mike to hold Yvonne while she fetched the nappy things and then, she says, Mike went on into bed. Kathleen changed Yvonne and brought her back to Joanne's bedroom. Joanne said she was going to go outside for a breath of fresh air; she was feeling hot and had been stuck inside all day and it might do her good.

Kathleen doesn't remember at what exact stage in these proceedings her mother went to bed. She remembers that after Joanne went out there was nobody in the kitchen.

Kathleen stayed a while in the bedroom with Yvonne and then she went to the empty kitchen. She opened the front door, peered into the darkness, saw nothing, called out to her sister and heard Joanne's reply from a distance that she would be in in a minute. Kathleen went back to the bedroom.

Immediately she heard Joanne come in she returned to the kitchen, which divides the bedrooms from the parlour and bathroom beyond.

Joanne had continued on to the bathroom. Kathleen saw drops of blood on the kitchen floor leading from the front door to the hot press and then from the hot press to the door that led to the bathroom.

Joanne came down that bathroom corridor now and appeared in the kitchen in a short-sleeved nightie. Over her arm was a blood-soaked nightdress. She said she'd had a heavy period and asked Kathleen if there were any sanitary towels. Kathleen said she hadn't any. Joanne went on through the kitchen and down the other corridor to her bedroom. Kathleen followed her. Joanne found sanitary towels in the wardrobe.

The two sisters lay down, Joanne on the bed, Kathleen on the mattress on the floor. She waited in the darkness for Joanne to speak, for Joanne to confirm what she suspected, that she had just had a baby. Joanne said nothing. There was silence, and eventually Kathleen fell asleep.

Joanne says she got up towards dawn, around half past five, and went out to where her now dead baby lay. It was in a pile of hay, about fifty yards from the house, close to the place where she had given birth. She saw, for the first time, that she had had a boy. She placed the baby in a brown paper bag and then in a plastic shopping bag, went down to the bedstead that acted as a gate, climbed over it and into another field, went to the end of that field to where the river was and hid the body of her child under a bramble ditch, near the river, in a pool of water that had overflowed.

She returned to bed and fell asleep.

When Kathleen woke up on that Friday morning, around eight o'clock, she went and helped Mike in the milking parlour. Then she woke her mother with a cup of tea. She told her mother that Joanne had had a miscarriage during the night, out in the field.

Kathleen brought Joanne a cup of tea. Joanne got up around ten o'clock. Kathleen saw her take a pair of tongs from the range and go out of the house. She stood at the front door and watched her go down the field and out of sight.

Kathleen went down the field a little, too. 'I did not know what I would find there, but I said I would go down and maybe I would find something.' She found two pools of blood in the grass. Under the hay nearby, she saw a plastic bag. She lifted the hay and the bag with her foot, and gravel poured out of the burst bag. 'I got afraid and I went up home.' She was afraid she'd see a baby. Joanne's mother got up and saw the drops of blood on the floor. She spoke to her daughter. Joanne said she had had a heavy period.

There was no discussion.

Words mean what you want them to mean.

Joanne haemorrhaged through that day and Kathleen went that night to her cousin for help. Joanne had words with her cousin, then with the doctor and then with the authorities in the hospital to which she was brought for treatment. She was sent home after seven days and nobody in authority said she'd had a baby.

The authorities said nothing at all to the family about it, whatever it was, and whatever it was was done with now. Their silence was an official sanction, and the family did not speak of whatever it was that had happened in the early hours of 13 April.

Nobody in the tribunal asked Joanne or Kathleen, during their long days of testimony, where Bridie Fuller was during the early hours of 13 April. She would have been due to get up around 1 am to keep nocturnal vigil, as she did every night in the kitchen. She would have been there when Joanne came in from the field in a blood-stained nightie dripping blood. Certainly she would have been there at dawn when Joanne got up to go back out to the field.

Bridie would surely have noticed something, and the

failure of the tribunal to ask Joanne and Kathleen about her was a startling one, but then the tribunal had other things on its mind. Public outrage about the nature of all the other questions put to Joanne Hayes had mounted to boiling point and the tribunal was under siege.

15. 'Please Sir?'

Three weeks had passed, there was no sign of the police being called to account for their actions and the tribunal was still mired in a squalid probe into the life of Joanne Hayes.

The mattress from her bed lay in a corner of the courtroom. The state of the sheets on which she had slept had been described by a forensic scientist, as had her nightdresses and her underwear. Her gynaecologist, John Creedon, had come into the tribunal and read out everything that had ever been recorded in her confidential records, including the dates and times of her menstrual flow since 1982, the width of her uterus after giving birth to Yvonne in 1983 and the kind of catgut used in suturing her afterwards. He described her vulva when he saw her again in hospital in April 1984, and the state her breasts might have been in, if he had examined them, was explored in detail, necessarily imaginative, by both him and the lawyers.

The judge had requested that a sample of blood be taken from one-year-old Yvonne, in a bid to trace her mother's previous sexual history. The tribunal was already in possession of the blood of Joanne Hayes.

When she took the stand Joanne Hayes was forced to give details of the exact date and place of the miscarriage that had taken place in 1982 and a description of the clots of blood that had seeped down her legs then in the toilet of the sports complex.

'When did you first make love?' she was asked. 'How long before Jeremiah Locke was it that you first had sex with somebody else?' Her belief that he was unhappy with his wife and would one day make a home with her attracted knowing scorn. That was the stuff of fairytales, 'like a prince finding the princess and putting her up on his white charger and riding off into the sunset'.

As for her thinking he would eventually go to her, would she care to define what 'eventually' meant? 'Never, I suppose,' she responded and was humbled. She was made to relive the Christmas night when she discovered that his wife, too, was pregnant, and he gave her short shrift; made to describe the 'quality of the pain' the day she went into labour in the farmhouse; asked to agree that 'you had no intention of allowing that child to be alive in this world after it left your body?' and forced to describe the appearance of the dead baby at dawn, 'crouched up or cold?' It was cold, she said.

She broke down repeatedly. Her tears and sobs and laboured breathing were a daily feature, an hourly feature and then a minute-by-minute occurrence as the interminable questions came at her in relays from the five legal teams gathered around her. Once there was a weekend break, and she came back with a mouth broken into sores and the judge observed that the weekend break hadn't done her any good. He saw no point in adjourning every time she broke down. 'If I rise now I will be rising every five minutes. Which is better, sooner or later?' The sooner they were done with her, the better for her and for them.

Before they were done with her, Joanne Hayes had a total collapse. She signalled its coming by asking the judge through tears, 'Please sir, may I go to the toilet?' He did not hear her. He was listening to her lawyer, who was on his feet and had precedence.

Dermot McCarthy pointed out that his client was under stress and needed to compose herself. 'She is going to remain under stress all morning and will have to do the best she can,' the judge replied. Brian Curtin whispered to Dermot McCarthy and Dermot McCarthy murmured to the judge that his client needed to go to the toilet. The judge then turned to her.

'Please sir?' she asked again.

He granted her request. She bolted from the court room. The tribunal adjourned. When it resumed, the judge was informed by a doctor that Joanne Hayes was in a state of acute anxiety. She was hyperventilating, vomiting, shaky and scarcely able to answer questions put to her. He had sedated her.

While they awaited her recovery, Kathleen Hayes was brought on to fill in the time. This tribunal was not going to waste a minute.

She said that the police had mocked her for having voted in favour of the pro-life amendment campaign, against abortion. It was nonsense to say that the police had brought religion into their interrogation of her, said police lawyer Anthony Kennedy.

He then questioned her about her Catholic attitude to the baby that she had suspected was lying somewhere out on the land. 'Did you think that it should get baptism? A Christian burial? The decency of a coffin and a consecrated grave?'

After lunch Kathleen was dismissed and Joanne Hayes brought back. The doctor had sedated her again over the lunch hour. She spoke at times with eyes closed, her head propped against the microphone. Her voice slurred.

At the end of the day the judge recommended that she receive further sedation to help her make it through the night. Her lawyers privately recommended that she should not go back to the farm. They asked that she be brought to Mary O'Riordan's house, where her friend could keep an eye on her. They were afraid that Joanne Hayes would commit suicide. It was so done.

The following morning, Mary O'Riordan remembers, Joanne came staggering into her bedroom, groggy and lost. Mary, her husband and Joanne had a good laugh about that. Then Mary brought Joanne to court, where she broke down again. Eventually Mary would not come to court any more. The phone calls she received in the middle of the night, anonymous, salacious and threatening, were too frightening.

Other people came, however, to picket the court. Joanne Hayes had by then spent longer in the witness box than any other person in the history of the Republic and had completed her testimony, but they wished to make their feelings clear. They wanted her and her family to know from whom the yellow flowers, telegrams, letters and Mass cards that deluged them had come.

16. Yellow Flowers

The first yellow flower was sent by Bernie McCarthy of the Tralee women's group, on Wednesday morning, 20 January at 11.15 am. She had come four miles into town from the country bungalow where she lived with her husband and three children. She was on her way to work, in Mahony's bookshop on the main street. She stopped off at an arcade where Jean Murphy ran a flower stall. Her instructions to Jean were meticulous: a single yellow flower, wrapped in cellophane, to be delivered to Joanne Hayes at the urban-council building where the court was sitting, before the one-thirty national radio news if possible. She wrote out a card, wishing luck to Joanne.

Later that morning two other women, expressing a similarly urgent desire, visited the florist.

Joanne Hayes emerged from the building at 1 pm bearing three yellow roses. Detailed testimony verging on the sordid had just been wrenched from her. The squalor of that detail, broadcast on the national news to people who were eating lunch and sitting with their families, was thrown into stark relief by the announcement that 'single yellow flowers' had been sent to Ms Hayes by women who wished her well.

The colour and the gesture gripped the imagination of listeners. Overnight, individually wrapped yellow flowers began to shower upon the woman impaled at the centre of the legal arena. It was not entirely spontaneous. A feminist network had fretted into action as Bernie McCarthy was making her way to the florist shop. A telephone call had gone from the Tralee women's group to an Irish feminist publishing group in

Dublin, which is housed in a building owned by the Irish Women Workers' Union. Róisín Conroy passed on the request, during a lunch-break discussion, to the various groups of women working in the building. One group consisted of eighteen women on the second floor who were participating in a training programme. The women ranged in age from twenty to forty-four and had thirty-five children between them and were all unemployed.

The price of a flower, less than two pounds, was just about manageable, and they all agreed to send one each. The request was passed up to the third floor, where another six women graduates of the first publishing course had set up their own Women's Community Press. An invitation to join in was sent to the office where a further five female officials worked.

Thirty roses were sent to Joanne Hayes. The order was placed with Interflora by Colette O'Neill, who had last attempted to directly influence the course of Irish history in 1971 as one of a group of women who took what has since become known as the 'Pill Train' to Northern Ireland, whence she brought back banned contraceptives. In that part of the island which is under British occupation, women enjoy a measure of control over their fertility. On her return to Dublin, armed with illegal contraband, Colette had declared to television cameras that 'The law is now obsolete.' Fourteen years later, as she ordered flowers for Joanne Hayes, the same law was still, with minor modifications, in force.

The telephone was then taken over by Sue Richardson of the Women's Community Press. She suspended work on her book on drug abuse, *Pure Murder*, the first ever publication to expose in depth the nature of the problem in Ireland. She began to make calls and to inform incoming callers that yellow roses were being sent to Joanne Hayes. Many of those phoning in asked to be put on the list. They would bring the money in when next they came to the building.

The situation called for trust. A hundred yellow roses had by now been ordered and the mainly poor women in the building would have to advance money for them. Their trust was not abused.

Throughout that day and the next, individual women from the three floors contacted their own groups back home. Each group was asked to send a flower and pass the message on to at least one more person. Catherine McConville rang the Sligo women's group which she had helped form only two years before. Scarcely had they come together than those women, hopeful, starry-eyed and in search of a brave new world, had come smack up against the pro-life campaign. Their nerve failed, as the nerve of so many women's groups had failed, and they had remained silent about the proposed amendment to the Constitution. They had barely stepped out into the world than they were slammed back behind closed doors, unable, as so few had been able, to bear the taunts and threats about women with murder in their hearts about the children in their wombs.

The Sligo women's group sent a shower of roses in response to the call from Catherine McConville.

The message had initially been taken by her husband, Declan Bree, father of two and the unemployed Independent Socialist member of Sligo County Council. He phoned Anne Gilmartin, a member of Catherine's group and also a member of the Labour Women's National Council, and she took over. Meantime Declan went down to The Terraces, a working-class street where the treasurer of his party lived. Brenda French's mother stood behind her at the front door. Both women gave him, at once, the price of two flowers. He spent the next couple of hours calling on people and collecting money.

Then he went into the shop of florist Kitty Maclarrick. She went into the back room and he heard her start to give painstaking instructions, over the phone, to a florist in Tralee, miles away. He heard her pause. 'Oh, you know all about it?'

he heard her say. The florist in Tralee, under siege, knew all about it.

Declan called into a café. The woman behind the desk was excited. 'Declan, there's a great plan. You have to send a yellow flower, just the one, to Joanne Hayes.' She had heard this from her brother's girlfriend. Declan Bree had left his home just four hours earlier to spread news of the plan and now he was being told about it on his return journey through that small town.

The Waterford resource centre received a call from Brigid Nevin, now working above in Dublin. Nadine Roche, who had worked for a time in Derry city, rang her former employers in the bookshop there. The Bookworm in turn rang another bookshop in Belfast. Galway had received a call from Sligo. Cork Quay Co-op and the Limerick Family Planning Centre were already saying 'We know, we know.' All of the women's groups listed in the annual *Irishwomen's Guidebook and Diary* were contacted.

Those telephoned were instructed to keep the flowers going to whichever member of the family took the stand after Joanne. All of those calls and all of those women are not, however, sufficient to account for the number of single yellow flowers that arrived for the Hayes family. It would be wishful thinking to conclude that there are that many active feminists in Ireland.

There were by now hundreds of flowers, bouquets, cards and letters arriving from all manner of people. Much of the correspondence was in the form of Mass cards. People whose heart went out to Joanne Hayes were nonetheless bewildered by the moral complexity of her situation.

17. Letters and Mass Cards

In Kerry, in January 1984, two people proclaiming devotion to the catholic faith came to public notice. One was Kevin McNamara, an elderly celibate prince of the Church who celebrated that month his promotion from bishop of Kerry to archbishop of Dublin. While he was being fêted, his parishioner Joanne Hayes, young, rural, unmarried, mother of one child, was being lacerated at the all-male tribunal.

'The central issue in The Kerry Babies case', said an editorial in the county newspaper, *The Kingdom*, 'is one that is as old as time itself . . . Falling in love can never be sufficient justification for the wilful destruction of the marriage bond . . . Up to now nobody – neither churchman nor statesman nor layman – has had the moral courage to call the Tralee affair by its proper name . . . the bishops and the pastors ought to be providing clear and unequivocal guidance. They ought to speak now or forever hold their peace.' Archbishop McNamara said nothing.

The people of the ninety-five-per-cent Catholic country said a lot. Joanne Hayes received more than five hundred letters, cards and notes which invoked, on her behalf, the intercession of a loving compassionate God who was clearly and with certainty seen to be quite a cut above the human metronomes who clocked up her imperfections. Irish Catholics, wanting genuinely to be good, struggling desperately under a yoke of bewildering rules and regulations, wrote to Joanne Hayes that no man should be allowed to sit in judgement on the human sexual condition.

Her ordeal called forth a confessional outpouring from women and men who had also suffered massively. They told her about themselves in letters; they told each other; all over the country the most amazing confidences were brought out and shared.

It was as though the great and fearful silence imposed by the amendment campaign was now being shattered as they called out that there were other truths that needed to be told, that it was all very well to revere and uphold the sanctity of life, but that life could break a person on the wheel and drive to very murder unless help was offered.

Their letters were a perfect cacophony of misery, anger and solidarity, and subjection to a God who alone could cope with what went on down here. The Catholics who wrote trusted God, not the priests nor the doctors nor the lawyers. As if to make the point more forcefully, one hundred and forty-two of the people who wrote to her enclosed Mass cards, indicating that human judgement had been bypassed in favour of a direct line to their God.

'The Holy Sacrifice of the Mass will be offered for your intentions to implore God's blessing', read the inscriptions. Unusually, the printed cards, normally held to be sufficient statements in themselves, bore scribbled insertions. 'No matter what you have done, any of us could have done the same in similar circumstances. Jesus loves you', said one. Another said 'I know you well now, with all I have read on the papers and seen on the telly. My heart goes out to you.'

Joanne Hayes's public suffering evoked memories of private ordeals and tribulations, striking chords in a population that had never been able to fully subscribe to the officially sanctioned norm. The letters showed that during her days on the stand people were literally sitting by their radios and televisions, confessing with her, hoping it would never happen to them, grieving that such personal matters should ever see the light of excruciating day.

'I have just heard on the news at 12 noon that your daughter has broken down while giving evidence. Will you tell her not to answer any more questions. May God help her, poor child', wrote a woman from County Cork. A Letterkenny lady wrote that 'my TV was broken but I watched on a neighbour's set. Your mother looks fed up and tired. If only she had your father's support. But he is in heaven praying for you all.' From Limerick came a card telling that 'I have just read a report of the questioning . . . it was the lowest, cruellest I have ever heard. I cried as I read it.' From the heart of bourgeois Dublin came a letter saying 'I cry as I think of how you are being hurt and I pray that Jesus will comfort you.' A bleakly beautiful reproduction of *Trees in the Snow* by William Leech bore the hopeless, affectionate message 'A wintry card for your wintry ordeal'. A Kilkenny woman declared that she would be down protesting, 'only for the bad roads'.

There was a sense of being trapped and helpless while Joanne Hayes was being legally crucified. A four-page letter told that the writer was snowed in, living on potatoes, out of cigarettes, and a mere two hundred yards from the nearest shop. 'It would be too dangerous to venture out.'

A signed Christmas card, full of incongruous good cheer and revelry, was sent by a policeman's wife who explained desperately that it was the only one she could get in a hurry.

The letters were shy and tactful, hoping she wouldn't mind strangers intruding on her already destroyed privacy. 'We hope you won't be offended by us writing to you but we thought you might like to know that there are many who are appalled', said one couple. A woman describing herself as a housewife and mother of three teenagers said, 'I want you to know that a lot of women everywhere are outraged at the way you are being treated. Sometimes it helps to know that someone out there cares and that everyone is not against you. I remember you every morning at Mass and always remember that God's love and mercy is greater than man's law.'

The letters sounded a resonant Catholic response to Christ's despairing cry 'Will you not watch one hour with me.' I stay awake at night; you are the last person I think of each night; my mother has been sending me reports of the tribunal; my thoughts are with you day and night; I have just heard on the Irish station in New York . . .

One Dublin family wrote to her several times, saying initially that the hurt she had suffered rendered them speechless, then that they were still too hurt and angry to say anything more, then sending her a Mass card, finally a card announcing that a whole series of Masses had been procured on her behalf.

Though commending her into God's hands, her correspondents were nevertheless thoughtful, argumentative and frank about her earthly situation. 'I am a married man with a lovely family and I love children as you do. We do not agree with sex outside marriage but God loves you.'

After having four children and finding herself pregnant again, she was 'too browned off' to go to a doctor and delayed seeking medical help until she was seven months pregnant, wrote one woman. She understood how hard it was in Joanne's case, 'the way things were for you'.

If she had ever intended hurting her baby she would have done so 'during the early stages', said another, referring discreetly to abortion. 'I believe things went wrong for you in the end . . . God loves you, regardless of the outcome.'

A signed note told that 'Life is very difficult and people make it harder for us. I had a hard life with a drunken gambling husband. I took a nervous breakdown and I am here in Donegal with my 86-year-old uncle. This last two and a half years I feel lonely. I wish I never got married. My God we women suffer through life, also the little girl in Granard last year, only a child.' A married woman in the Midlands said she had only lately begun to understand her husband's favourite saying that 'an erect penis has no conscience. How I would love to make young girls understand that just because a man wants to go to bed with them does not mean that he loves them. Too, too late so many of us have brokenheartedly learnt that. We are inclined to condemn the male instinct and yet both instincts are God given and therefore right. 'Tis what we sometimes do with them that brings trouble. I also pray for Jer Locke and his family. What a start to a marriage which as you know Mrs Hayes is never easy anyway, however worthwhile. Poor Johanna, how often the woman is made feel guilty and yet we are all individuals with free will. Before the Christ who died for me I cannot blame anyone else for what I've done and before Christ the man cannot try to blame the woman, even though from Adam it is tried.'

Two single mothers wrote a joint letter. 'Thousands of girls go to England for abortions and of those who freely admit it not one is subjected to the least bit of criticism. Enclosed is a cardigan for Yvonne. It should fit until she's two and a half.' He had left Kerry in the Fifties, wrote an elderly man, fallen in love with the wrong person, 'and am now paying the penalty for my mistakes and probably will for the rest of my life. It involves divorce, abortion and other tragedies. I know your home village very well, and the surrounding villages, Lixnaw, Kilflynn and Tralee. May God help you, you deserve a break.'

A Kilkenny women said 'My little girl is just four. She knows you on the paper and TV and she wonders about the babies. I am an unwed mum too. May God guide you on the right road. All I can do is pray for all concerned.'

A former IRA man from Galway wrote that he had contacted a former IRA woman in Dublin, 'asking her to organise the young women of Dublin, as she did in the twenties. I was happy and proud when I saw on the television what those Kerry women did outside the tribunal.'

A County Cork woman recommended prayer to Padre Pio. 'I had been suffering from lumps on both breasts for 2 years, going in and out of hospital monthly. The specialist told me the lumps had taken a turn and I should have both breasts removed right away. Well, Joanne, only for St Martin and Padre Pio I'd be gone queer in the head. Now I have a clot as well under my right arm. I know these are very different circumstances to you, but God only knows what I went through and St Martin and Padre Pio helped me, when I could cry at a minute's notice. Forgive me for writing but I hope one day you'll be the happiest person in the whole world. The wheels don't ever stop turning, and St Martin and Padre Pio won't let you down.'

She had a marvellous husband who wasn't in the least worried about her past, wrote a woman who hoped that Joanne would be similarly blessed. She recommended Psalm 139, 'O Lord, you search me and know me'. A mother whose teenage daughter had been killed in a car crash said that she often went to the foot of the Blessed Virgin in the church and prayed for strength. 'Joanne, you pray too to your little boy in Heaven. But for the narrow minded people of Ireland, holy Ireland at that, your little boy would be alive today, as you wouldn't be afraid of being a mother.'

Whether she gave birth inside or outside the house, 'God bless you. You made a mistake. Don't do so again', wrote a Clare woman. No matter what she had done, any of us could have done the same in similar circumstances, a correspondent underlined every scribbled word in the Mass card. Several urged, in kindly tones, the use of contraception. If the tribunal could prove that a woman could have twins by two different men, one twin obviously born some time after the other, she would eat her typewriter, a woman threatened.

'I used to feel that you must be very hard to neglect your baby, in the pregnancy and birth, but now I understand your actions more clearly I think. It seems to me that when you realised things weren't going to work out you just stopped thinking about your pregnancy as a baby', a stranger wrote.

'If the baby was born in the house don't be afraid to say it. Our Lady will help you', came a letter from a nurse. A mother said, 'If I can console you at all with a bit of information relating to the birth of my first child in hospital, the nurse pulled the cord and it broke before the afterbirth was delivered.'

Who did what, or where, inside or outside the house, was not important, came a signed letter from a family that was praying for her. A bunch of neighbours from a street in Cork told her she was 'God's child, and should you have erred what harm. We all do at some time in our lives. Not one of us would know what way we would react if we were placed in a similar position.'

A woman from Donegal asked for help in dealing with 'my husband – my beast'. She wrote several times, each letter unfolding a chapter of misery. A doctor wrote from a psychiatric hospital where he had signed himself in to get away from his wife. 'You are paying the price of reform for all of us. Thank you. God bless you all', said a well-wisher.

There was an astonishing amount of correspondence from nuns. One said 'Tell the truth anyway, Joanne, no matter what. I thank God that the Lord is our judge and he judges the heart, not the actions. That's where he differs from the human judges – they can only judge actions, which leaves a lot to be desired. Be strong. We are backing you with much prayer these days.'

A nun wrote from a Kildare convent that 'I'm suffering terribly myself, Joanne. I've been sinful sexually and I'm so proud before God to be one of his forgiven sinners. I am a woman. I pain for you. I pray for you. I understand you. You have suffered so much – a mother losing a baby, a lover paining with pain for the man you loved, the probable pain of guilt and shame, the bodily pain of birth, the public scorn and misunderstanding, the spiritual nameless suffering of going against social mores. Love from your sister in suffering.'

A nun on spiritual retreat told her that the priest directing the retreat had asked for prayers for the Hayes family. A nun travelled to Tralee to present a card signed by all the sisters in her Dublin convent.

Group support was expressed in telegrams by the Ennis soroptimist club; the women's department of Sinn Féin; the female attendants of St Fintan's hospital, Portlaoise; Family Aid; the principal and staff of Dunlavin National School; the ladies' club, Dundalk; the Dublin inner-city project; workers in a Galway office; thirty-one villagers from Maam Cross, County Galway; the staff of AFRI, a Third World organisation; female telephonists in the Galway exchange; the staff and managing director of Unisex hair salon in County Kildare; sixteen teachers from Killester Vocational School, Dublin; the Connolly Youth Movement; the Kilrush Tenants' Association, County Clare; the Limerick office staff of the Irish Transport and General Workers' Union; the NUJ chapel of *City Limits* magazine, London; the Galway civil rights group; a self-help women's group in Cork; and the Labour women's national council.

18. Abbeydorney Comes to Town

Long before the tribunal began, the signpost to Abbeydorney was daubed with graffiti. Rivulets of paint ran down from the letters of the superimposed word so that 'Sex' dribbled straight into 'Abbeydorney'. The rural villages of small-town Ireland had been invisibly tarred with the same brush since the novel *Valley of the Squinting Windows* was published in 1918. It told a story of gossip, scandal and silence and it became the bible of outsiders who wondered what went on in small communities.

The graffito has since been removed from the signpost. The novel is now considered an outdated document. Abbeydorney changed everything when it came marching into Tralee in support of Joanne Hayes. Those who saw the villagers standing silently with placards outside the court sensed the turning of a page of history.

The idea of protesting came to John Barrett when he read an account of the tribunal in the *Irish Press*. The paper quoted a farmer from Rathmore on the county border who had been sent into court by his neighbours to see for himself what was going on and report back. Rathmore has not forgotten the mentally retarded man who was convicted of a sex-murder on the evidence of a policeman who hid under his bed and claimed to have overheard an incriminating conversation. The Rathmore farmer was so incensed by the tribunal and by the sedation of Joanne Hayes, which he had witnessed, that he was going home to get 'the pike out of the thatch'. The phrase is honoured code for rural rebellion.

John Barrett is a man of standing in Abbeydorney. His father had captained the football team which brought the All-Ireland Sam Maguire cup to Kerry for the first time. As a former sub-editor on a national newspaper and now contributor of a sports column to *Kerry's Eye*, John Barrett had a shrewd nose for newsmaking.

He telephoned Jerome Donovan, the enormously popular village butcher who had stood bail for Joanne Hayes in the sum of five thousand pounds when she was first arrested. He had also promised to meet the family's legal bill, should the case ever come to trial, sharing costs with their cousin Paudie Fuller, a Fianna Fáil councillor.

No one in Abbeydorney thought the charges would ever be sustained in court. Now they were witnessing a trial within a tribunal. Between them, John Barrett and Jerome Donovan rang every villager and farmer within the parish who had a telephone. Within two hours of that Tuesday afternoon's work they were confident enough to place an order with the publishers of *Kerry's Eye* for the immediate printing of streamers that said 'Abbeydorney supports Joanne'.

Some of the villagers went into Tralee at an early hour on Wednesday morning to pick up the streamers and staple them onto cardboard placards. The farmers came as soon as they had done their milking. They were all on the picket line by nine o'clock. The frost hadn't melted off the roads and the tribunal was not due to start until ten o'clock.

Newspapers that morning had given a front-page lead to criticism of the tribunal by the national parliament's Committee on Women's Rights. While John Barrett and Jerome Donovan had been telephoning neighbours, the TDs (members of parliament) had been telling each other in committee that it was time for the minister for justice, Michael Noonan, to intervene in the tribunal. They described the cross-examination as 'insensitive', 'very, very frightening', 'harrowing and quite horrific' and 'shameful'.

The tribunal, said the all-party committee, showed an attitude to women's sexuality that needed to be examined. People involved in counselling rape victims had indicated to them that the 'interrogation' of rape victims was similar. The 'manner and matter, tone and tenor' of the tribunal 'would fundamentally affect people's attitudes to women'.

The Abbeydorney villagers said nothing; their presence said everything to the world's media who had come to televise them. After two hours of walking silently up and down, they went into the council building and stood around the walls of the packed court. Kathleen Hayes was on the stand.

In a room set specially aside for members of the family Joanne Hayes sat with her daughter Yvonne and brother Ned. The villagers came in to see them and were introduced to workers from the sports complex who had also come to keep vigil.

Cups of tea were taken in an atmosphere of strained courtesy as town and country met. Yvonne became the focus of a conversation that never once took account of the legal horror next door. When Kathleen came off the stand and a lunch break was called, the villagers went home as quietly and purposefully as they had come. The valley of the squinting windows was no more.

19. Protest

The Abbeydorney demonstration was followed next day by a feminist demonstration that drew participants from all over the country. Dawn streaked the sky as women shivered outside a city-centre Dublin store that had bowed to the recession and closed. The women had one thing in common – financial poverty. They were full-time mothers, or unemployed radicals, or graduates on the dole.

Kate Shanahan, who had co-ordinated the trip from the women's centre in Dame Street, thought that between them the fifty-four women could cobble together the £225 it cost to hire the bus they now waited for. Her own group, Women for Disarmament, had contributed forty pounds and was sponsoring three travellers. The bus didn't come.

When offices opened for business at 9 am she began to ring bus-hire firms. The women were tired, hungry and irritable and they hadn't even begun the two-hundred-mile journey yet. They had come into the city from the outlying suburbs of Tallaght, Clondalkin and Ballymun, or from flatland, and most of them had been up since 6 am, preparing food for children whom they would leave behind with husbands or friends, making sandwiches for their own journey, going out then into the streets in winter pitch darkness to catch an early bus or share a taxi.

At ten o'clock a coach was procured from CIÉ (the public-transport system) at a cost of £320, one hundred pounds more than anticipated. As it moved out of the city, coins and notes were collected and still they were thirty pounds short.

There was only one woman on that coach in possession of a cheque book and she stopped at a rural town to draw out sufficient money to make up the difference, on the understanding that it would some day be repaid into her overstretched account after someone had organised a fund-raising event. Weeks later this was done.

At Newbridge, County Kildare, they picked up three women who had waited faithfully in the certain knowledge that the women's bus would turn up some time. In Portlaoise at noon, three hours behind schedule, they picked up a woman who had waited outside the prison all morning. Patricia Bennet had kidney trouble but she had not dared, during all that time, to leave the designated rendezvous and go in search of a toilet. Portlaoise prison houses the country's political prisoners and the police and army had viewed with alarm the solitary woman opposite their main gates who kept peering anxiously up the main road to Dublin. They had several times asked her to move on. She cheered, and the women cheered, as the bus finally pulled in. Apart from that communal outbreak of emotional solidarity, though, the passengers kept quietly to their own groups of friends.

'There was no singing, no political oratory, no sloganeering on the way to Tralee,' says Kate Shanahan. The passengers were drawn from all political groups and from none, from Sinn Féin, Revolutionary Struggle, the Socialist Workers' Movement and Liberation for Irish Lesbians to the women of KLEAR who are teaching themselves how to read and write and who were on their first-ever demonstration.

'There was no effort at a quick teach-in. There was no need. We had one thing in common and that was that we were women. It was the only thing we had in common. It was more than enough. That bus was fuelled by anger. You could feel it. It was a speechless anger and it was sad and no analysis that any political section could offer would have been big enough to encompass it.' Joanne Hayes, they felt, had undergone agonising scrutiny simply because she was a woman. The perfect excuse had been found to pin a woman under the microscope and have a good look at her. She had been charged with no crime, but womanhood itself was on trial in Tralee.

When the bus arrived in Tralee, there were already hundreds of women and quite a few men parading in front of the council buildings. Kate Shanahan was as surprised as Marguerite Egan was delighted. This demonstration was unlike any other demonstration that seasoned feminists had attended. 'There were ordinary people in it!' says Marguerite Egan.

Their own mothers were out there with them. Kate's mother, who lives in Tralee, was waiting for the Dubliners with that most traditionally motherly of sights, an armful of food. 'She had used four sliced pans to make sandwiches, including vegetarian sandwiches, for she knew that some of my friends didn't eat meat. I had thought that she might bring me a snack and then disappear after saying hello to me, but she came on the demo with us and she said her heart soared when she saw us pouring out of the bus. She thought that only a few of us would have bothered when it came to the crunch, and that's why she only used four sliced pans.'

There were matrons from Castlemaine, complete with banner, neighbouring women from Abbeydorney, a busload of women from Cork, a carload from Belfast and hundreds from Tralee itself. 'When Joanne came out of the building we were awestruck. The size of her struck everybody. We couldn't believe she was so small,' says Kate Shanahan. 'And then her mother came out. That nearly wrecked us. She looked so ordinary. She looked like a, like a . . . mother. And we stared at them for a while, all of us raving feminists, and these ordinary shy country people, and we had come all the way to support them and now we didn't want to intrude. There was this gulf between us, between our experience and theirs, our beliefs and theirs, just a big gulf and we wanted to reach across it and say we're all ordinary. We didn't. We didn't know how to do it, what would be the right gesture.'

An old woman stepped out of the crowd which lined the footpath and went right up and hugged Mary Hayes. 'It felt great. It looked right. One old woman hugging another.' The younger women held back from reaching out to Joanne. 'There was this big sense that we didn't wanted to intrude. Her privacy had been invaded enough. So we just looked at her, like fools, and held out our flowers and cards to her, and she couldn't take them. Her arms were already full of them. We loaded up Kathleen, she was a bit overcome by it all, crying and smiling, and then Ned and Mike.'

The Hayeses disappeared into the hotel opposite and then the lawyers came out. 'A woman behind me was yelling "Bastard" at this man in a suit and someone pointed out that it was Joanne's solicitor Patrick Mann. It was just one man in a suit after another, and then came the judge in his suit. We lined up and booed him. He had this little smile on his face.'

When the building had emptied and there seemed nothing else to do – all that journeying from all over Ireland to speak their minds and show their feelings, and now it was over inside half an hour – the pent-up energy was suddenly released in the direction of the police station, just down the road.

'A crowd gathers its own momentum,' says Kate Shanahan. 'Next thing we knew we were outside the barracks and you could tell the non-political people. They were the ones with the bemused looks on their faces.' One incident on the way there had cheered her up. An elderly countryman in a dark-blue serge suit had danced in rage up to the two young men in the forefront of the procession and said, 'Let the women out in front. It's their day.' She wondered if Ireland would ever be the same again.

Outside the station a woman from Revolutionary Struggle started chanting through a loud hailer 'Kennedy, Courtney, both start shaking, today's pigs are tomorrow's bacon'. The crowd started drifting off to a pub which had been hired for the night and some women went back to the hotel for the scheduled press conference.

There were only four reporters there. The other journalists had caught the evening train to Dublin. Miriam Killeny was glad of their absence. The representative of Cherish, the first group ever formed in the country to fight specifically for the rights of unmarried mothers, had failed to arrive in Tralee. She had been plucked out of the crowd to read a statement on its behalf. 'Someone came racing along asking for a single mother, any single mother, to speak for Cherish.'

After the conference Miriam went downstairs to the bar. 'The Hayes family were sitting at a table on their own. The whole thing looked odd. We had come from all over to support them and now we couldn't even speak to each other. We were constantly held back by a sense of not wanting to intrude, but if we didn't go over it might look as though we were using them, as though they were a handy peg on which to hang the feminist cause.'

Two women eventually approached the family and Mary Hayes said they were grand to have come all that way to Tralee in that weather. The gulf was bridged.

'Mary Hayes would leave a lump in your throat. Her sons and daughter were around her, still full of youth, but there she was, on in years, up to her neck in trouble when she should have been looking forward to retirement, just like my own mother,' says Kate Shanahan. 'And then you'd think of your own mother. If any one of us were put on public exhibition, what family would come through unblemished? You'd look at Mary Hayes and know that every mother in the country had escaped trauma by a wing and a prayer. She was the one that got picked out. Going back on the bus that night I bet every woman was thinking of her own mother, and how close we all are to disaster if the public should be given a look in at us.'

The women arrived back in Dublin at three in the morning. The conductor left them as near to their homes as he could. In the middle of the night they set off in pairs and threes, to hitch and walk, those who lived far away benefiting from yet another collection of shillings to get a taxi home.

When the tribunal resumed the following Monday, Justice Kevin Lynch spoke his mind on the scenes of the previous week.

20. Scramble to the Hospital

I

On Monday morning, 28 January, Judge Kevin Lynch opened up proceedings with a bombastic attempt to assert authority over a tribunal that seemed to the public to have gone out of control. Parliamentarians had been freely critical, the villagers of Abbeydorney had marched on him, feminists had surrounded him and the police into whose behaviour he had been enquiring had been photographed offering him protection.

The judge described the women as 'raucous, ignorant urban dwellers' and he threatened jail sentence on anyone who, in his opinion, insulted or obstructed the tribunal. He personally would impose the sentence, up to a maximum of two years, and he personally would decide if the person who committed contempt and subsequently sought release from jail were sincerely and sufficiently apologetic, and he would be in no personal hurry to hear apologies, since he was a busy man.

The public did not know what they were talking about, he said. They had not seen the files, which he described as 'the founts of wisdom and knowledge'. (He was referring to files such as those written by Detective Sergeant P.J. Browne, who had said 'This is the sad story of a woman scorned . . .')

The judge then remarked to Dermot McCarthy that he had seen, over the weekend, a newspaper photograph of Bridie Fuller sitting at home with her family. When did she propose to appear before the tribunal? Mr McCarthy promised to look into the matter.

That afternoon Bridie Fuller was removed to hospital, suffering from a second stroke. The court was not told, nor was any sick certificate produced. On Wednesday morning, 30 January, the judge returned to the subject again. He had heard, he said, that Bridie Fuller was now in hospital.

Mr McCarthy agreed.

He was sure, said the judge, that Mr McCarthy was most anxious that Miss Fuller should give evidence.

Mr McCarthy agreed.

He understood, said the judge, that when Miss Fuller had been similarly indisposed before, she had merely found difficulty in walking, but that her intellect was unaffected.

The two men discussed whether some day Bridie Fuller might be able to negotiate the front steps of this or any other court venue. They agreed it would be exceedingly difficult. The judge revealed that he had, unknown to anybody else, personally checked the back entrance to the court. Although the services of his tipstaff were available to him, and those of his legal team, and indeed those of any doctor in the land, this High Court judge had taken upon himself the humble and secret task of walking up and down the back stairwell of the court, trying to figure out if an old, ill and halt woman could somehow be hauled up its narrow length and brought before him.

He had figured out that this couldn't be done either, the judge informed Mr McCarthy. He then broke the stalemated silence with a rush of words. He was adjourning at once, immediately and without delay to the hospital, and the lawyers, guards, journalists and public could join him there. Judge Lynch rose and was gone. There followed the kind of scene which he had warned against on Monday, when he had said 'This tribunal shall not be insulted'. In the mad scramble to get to the hospital, the tribunal insulted itself, as startled lawyers ran, walked and tumbled out of the courthouse, to stand on the steps and ask 'Which hospital, where, when, how shall we get there?' Tralee had three hospitals, the old and the new and the home for the elderly. A television crew were well on the road to Killarney, where Bridie had previously stayed, before caution persuaded them to come back and at least check out her home town.

Taxis were commandeered, passing motorists were begged for lifts, cars were dangerously packed with strangers who had abandoned all pretence at legal dignity in the scramble to get to God knows where in a town with which they were unfamiliar.

One journalist seized the opportunity to get into a cab and issue the immortal line, 'Follow that judge.'

Two feminists set off on one man's borrowed bike.

At the hospital the rudely healthy visitors were packed into a teaching annexe. Nurses came across the lawn with trays of water and glasses. Uneasy jokes were cracked about 'Scotch and ice'. Would Bridie testify from an oxygen tent, surpassing the spectacle of Joanne Hayes testifying under sedation?

The judge came in and sat down and Dermot McCarthy admitted for the first time that he was representing a woman he had not met. 'I have not had an opportunity to have consultations with her.' Consultant physician Robert McEneaney took the oath and told the assembly that Bridie Fuller was paralysed and brain-damaged and totally unable to testify. The tribunal proceeded to establish just what kind of brain damage Bridie had. 'There are different types of brain damage,' said Martin Kennedy. 'There is brain-damage which renders one less capable of intellectual capacity and brain damage which does not.'

Bridie Fuller had both, they were told. Her comprehension was quite good, but her ability to express ideas was impaired, as was her ability to speak.

'A person with a stammer may have difficulty in speaking, but no difficulty in formulating ideas.' Martin Kennedy seized on the notion that Bridie could think, whatever her little difficulty about expressing those thoughts. The spectre arose of a tribunal conducted through sign language.

Bridie had difficulty even in formulating ideas, he was told. Anthony Kennedy wanted to know if alcohol was a factor. The spectre arose of Bridie Fuller skulking in the hospital with a hangover.

Alcohol was not a factor in her condition, he was assured. 'Do you think she would be in a position to understand legal advice?' asked Mr McCarthy.

'No,' said the doctor.

'Would she be able to receive advice sufficiently to make a will?' asked the judge.

'Possibly, yes,' said the doctor.

The only problem really about giving advice, summed up the judge, was the physical problem of talking and that might be resolved as Ms Fuller's health improved. 'We do not need to have her capable of walking.'

Turning to Mr McCarthy he warned 'Insofar as receiving instructions is concerned, this is the middle of the fourth week we are in Tralee and she has been out and about during that time and there is going to be no delay once I get word that this lady is fit . . .'

The tribunal made its way back to Tralee. There was humiliation in the air.

II

Bridie Fuller was not a talkative person. Since her premature retirement in 1969, when she was fifty-four years old, she had withdrawn gradually into a world of her own, sleeping by day, sitting wakefully by the range in the kitchen all through the night. After giving up her car, due to what her loyal family resolutely refused to call a drink problem, she withdrew even more from the real world of other people.

To outsiders, she appeared strange, even neglected. The peace commissioner before whom she was brought in the special court in the garda station said she looked as though she hadn't been washed since Christmas. To family and friends, she was a woman who commanded, when in the full of her health, massive respect, and who was given, as her mind and body declined, deep affection. They accepted her as she was and chose not to disturb her.

Not an eyebrow was raised when Bridie turned up once at the funeral of a former nursing colleague, in a state of disarray. She joined the guard of honour wearing her old uniform. She had put the uniform on over her civilian clothes, which hung down below the hem. A tattered cardigan, pulled on over the lot, completed the ensemble.

Those who saw her that day remembered the military precision that Bridie had brought from her career in the British army to civilian nursing in Tralee. If the working day began at nine in the morning, Bridie used to arrive in hospital at twenty minutes before the hour.

She would take off her coat, fold her nursing cardigan over her arm, light a cigarette and sit up straight in her chair as she smoked. All around her other nurses would be slumped in chairs, unwilling to move until the hands of the clock should meet on the hour. Bridie got to her feet at ten to nine, put out her cigarette and reported early for duty.

Now, here she was, retired and bedraggled at the guard of honour. Her colleagues were still honoured to have her. Sister Aquinas tried once in a while to comb Bridie's hair, one elderly sister tending another, and accepted the irritated rebuff without rancour. Then they would sit together by the range, silently, Bridie responding to the simple questions put to her: had she slept well, was she eating? Bridie was famous in Abbeydorney for only ever volunteering one piece of conversation. 'What time is it?' she would ask. On being told, she would lapse again into silence.

She did not read newspapers, or listen to the radio or watch the television. She could not make a cup of tea.

In the police station, on 1 May, she had sat from twelve noon until ten at night, saying virtually nothing, responding as best she could to the polite chit-chat manufactured by the guards who came to sit with her throughout the day. She did not know that Joanne was pregnant, she answered their repeated questions.

Then Joanne was brought down to see her.

The guards acknowledge that Joanne was in tears. They record that Joanne said to Bridie: 'I was talking to Liam Moloney and I told him the truth.'

Joanne Hayes had told Liam Moloney that she gave birth in the field. Liam Moloney acknowledges that he forgot to get her to sign that statement. When he brought it to her for signature after she had confessed to murdering the Cahirciveen baby, she had tapped the paper with her hand, he said, and declared 'This is the truth.' Now, however, in the garda station she said to Bridie, 'You were in the room, Bridie. I told them.' Bridie would not have been released from the station unless she implicated herself, was how Joanne Hayes later explained these words.

Bridie made a statement saying she had delivered the child in the farmhouse.

Bridie Fuller never retracted that statement and never accused the guards of pressurising her in any way to make it. When the family went to see their solicitor Patrick Mann to explain what had happened to them, Bridie sat in a silence that was occasionally broken by a mumble. 'I got the impression,' he said later, 'that if you told Bridie the cow jumped over the moon, Bridie would repeat that the cow jumped over the moon.'

Bridie did once refer to the matter, during the summer, when Sister Aquinas came to visit her. She was looking upset and the nun asked her 'What's the matter, Bridie, were you involved?' Sister Aquinas was talking about the birth of Joanne's baby, the circumstances of which were still unclear to her. 'No,' said Bridie, 'but I changed my statement. I thought it would help Joanne.' The nun said nothing. She did not want to upset Bridie further, she said. Besides which, she herself was upset.

Bridie had also raised the topic with her old nursing colleague, Kathleen Ferry, who came to look after her during the days when the family was attending the tribunal. She said to Ms Ferry, 'I want to tell you what happened.' Ms Ferry said 'Don't be upsetting yourself, Bridie, don't bother your head about all that.' After a few minutes Bridie raised her head and asked, 'What time is it?'

When the charges were dropped in October 1984, Bridie Fuller was in hospital with a stroke. The internal police inquiry was unable to take a statement from her, but that did not matter, since the police were interested mainly in how the family had come to confess to stabbing the Cahirciveen baby, and Bridie had not implicated herself in that.

Bridie spent the winter in three hospitals, in Cork, Killarney and Tralee. When she recovered mobility, she was sent home. She was under strict instructions to continue taking tablets for the high blood pressure that was starving her brain of oxygen. Between Christmas and the opening of the tribunal in Tralee, on 7 January, a leading criminal lawyer received a phone call from Patrick Mann asking him to represent the family. The lawyer was given to understand that he would not be able to talk to all the family before the proceedings opened. One of them was incoherent. The lawyer declined to represent a family whose full story he did not know.

Bridie did not come to the tribunal. Her family felt that she would never be well enough to come. Joanne and Kathleen discussed with Patrick Mann the necessity of getting a sick certificate that would excuse her. A physician in Tralee hospital, whom Patrick Mann recommended, said that if Bridie was reasonably well in body, she could only be excused by a psychiatrist, which he was not, and he refused to examine her.

The family doctor, Liam Hayes, who had never noticed that Joanne was pregnant, had by now left Tralee to practise elsewhere. Joanne told Patrick Mann that she did not feel like asking Dr Hayes's partner Dr Daly to come and see Bridie. Her previous experience of asking him for help and being told that he might involve the police had soured her.

Dr Francis Chute, a general practitioner, agreed to go out to the farmhouse to see her. Bridie was by then refusing to take her tablets. He cajoled her into resumption of medication by talking about the old times they had spent together in hospital, twenty years ago. He did not medically examine her. He rang Patrick Mann that evening and told him that, as he was not Bridie's family doctor and had not examined her, he was unable to issue a certificate excusing attendance at the tribunal.

The family could not afford a psychiatrist and her lawyers, operating on a shoestring, did not hire one.

The tribunal sat from 7 January until 28 January, with no sign of Bridie Fuller and no medical certificate to excuse her. None of her three legal representatives – Patrick Mann, Brian Curtin, junior counsel, and Dermot McCarthy, senior counsel – had been to see her. Officially, therefore, they were representing a woman whose version of events was a direct contradiction of that offered by their other clients, her relatives. For all they knew, she might stick by her statement to the police. That statement was part of the judge's fount of wisdom and knowledge. Unlike the public, he was obliged to keep an open mind. The missing witness, as he had demonstrated by his dash to the hospital, was preying on it.

21. Sister's Testimony

Seven days later, on Wednesday 6 February, Bridie Fuller was adjudged fit, and the tribunal returned to the hospital. Before it did so, however, Michael Hayes told it that Joanne Hayes gave birth, not in the field, but in her bedroom.

Michael Hayes is educationally subnormal.

He had spent two days in the witness box saying that he had not known Joanne was pregnant. In the closing minutes of his testimony, he was questioned by James Duggan, junior counsel on the judge's legal team.

Did he know what an oath was? No.

Mr Duggan read it out to him.

Had it been explained to him in primary school? No.

Had he not been told that he was calling Almighty God down to stand beside him? No.

Unable to rely totally on God's help, the lawyer invoked the name of Mike's beloved sister. Kathleen, 'a very truthful person, she doesn't tell lies', had said under oath that in her opinion all the family had known, before Mike found the baby in the field, that Joanne had given birth.

'Where was that child born? In what room?' the lawyer ran the two questions together in natural sequence. 'In the top room. Above my room,' the youth responded. In Joanne's room. Naturally.

Had Mike been there? No.

Had Kathleen been there? No.

Had Bridie been there? No.

The careful lawyer did not ask if Joanne herself had been there.

'Did Joanne give birth on her own?' Yes.

Who had told Mike about this and when? 'I think it was Kathleen, going down the field, going down the field where Joanne told her the baby was.'

Was it then that Kathleen told him that Joanne had given birth in the room? 'No, I did not hear her say that at all.'

After the court then, before going down the field, the lawyer cajoled, Kathleen 'at that stage told you Joanne had given birth to the child in the room. Is that right?' Yes, said Mike simply.

Mike, said the judge, had placed the birth in the room 'only after he had been reminded in the most specific terms of the meaning and solemnity of the oath'.

That evening the Hayes family were asked by their lawyers if they would agree to have Mike examined by a psychiatrist and the results read out in court. In the absence of any formal certification, newspapers were bound to report Michael, and the tribunal was bound to regard him as being of adult intelligence. It was rather like closing the stable door after the horse had bolted.

There was no time to arrange for a psychiatrist to see Bridie. The very next morning physician Robert McEneaney indicated privately that Bridie Fuller was sufficiently recovered to testify. The judge announced that no members of the public would be allowed into the hospital and he restricted access to four journalists.

Unlike the previous occasion, the tribunal did not sit in a distant annexe. The precaution was taken of keeping Bridie in the main building, in a room only seconds away from life-saving machines. A nurse brought in Bridie Fuller in a wheelchair and stayed by her side.

Dermot McCarthy now saw and heard her for the first time. He had no more idea than anyone else what she was going to say. Patrick Mann had instructed him, on the way to the hospital, that Bridie would receive key words, like a machine. Whatever was punched in would come out. Sister Aquinas offered the same opinion of Bridie's mental state. 'She had made this statement [to the guards] and I see it as a kind of record inside her mind, probably troubling her, and that having made the statement she just held on to it.'

Mr Justice Lynch opened proceedings by telling Bridie that the government had asked him to investigate the birth of Joanne's baby. The government had asked him to investigate an awful lot more than that, but presumably he wanted to keep things simple. 'You don't worry. You do the best you can. Nobody will be hard on you or rude to you.' The language was reminiscent of a parent talking to a child.

He cautioned the lawyers to 'adopt a chatty pose'. Anthony Kennedy, normally wont to ask witnesses to 'stop acting the gom', chatted Bridie up a storm. 'I will start by telling you,' he said, 'something very nice that was said about you yesterday.' He was sure, he said, that Bridie Fuller would be delighted to know that a certain person had told 'the judge and everybody else what a grand nurse you were.' This person had even 'said out loud that you were a first-rate nurse . . . I am sure that pleases you?' Mr Kennedy, the judge told the old woman, 'is a very nice man'.

The judge's senior counsel Michael Moriarty got right down to business.

'What we heard from your nephew, Michael Hayes, is that a birth took place in Joanne's room in the farmhouse in Abbeydorney,' he said. He did not say that they had also heard from Joanne, Mary, Kathleen and Ned Hayes that the birth took place in the field. Mr Moriarty kept things simple.

'Yes,' said Bridie.

'Could you tell us what you remember about that birth taking place on that night?'

'I remember,' said Bridie, 'she was pregnant and she delivered herself that night.'

'We heard yesterday from Mike,' Mr Moriarty persisted, 'that in fact the child was born in her bedroom on the farm. Would that be right?'

'Yes,' agreed Bridie.

'It was in her bedroom,' Mr Moriarty said. He had now punched that home three out of four times and Bridie Fuller had merely agreed with what was put to her.

During her two sessions of testimony, lasting one and a half hours each, on that Wednesday and the following Friday, Bridie Fuller agreed with whatever version was presented to her by individual lawyers, each version being different.

The following exchanges took place on the cutting of the umbilical cord:

Moriarty: Were you able to do anything yourself in relation to the umbilical cord?

BF: No.

Seconds later it was discussed again.

Moriarty: What way did you help? Did you cut it?

BF: Just cut it, got a scissors.

McCarthy: Did they [the guards] suggest to you that you cut the cord?

BF: Yes.

McCarthy: Did they suggest that to you?

BF: No, I said it myself.

She had broken the waters, she did not break the waters, yes she did break the waters. She had washed the baby, she did not wash the baby, she had washed every orifice in the baby's body. She had been in the room only once, no twice, no three times, definitely only four times, definitely only five times, she made a last visit on the sixth occasion, no she had definitely paid a last visit on the seventh occasion. The longer the lawyers stayed in Bridie's room, the longer Bridie stayed in Joanne's room. The longer she stayed there, the more she became confused.

She even agreed with Martin Kennedy's theory about twins. 'Is it possible that Joanne had a baby that night about half-eleven or twelve o'clock, while you were asleep in your bed?'

BF: How?

MK: . . . twins.

BF: . . . twins?

MK: . . . twins.

BF: She might have.

A major influence on the public understanding that Bridie Fuller's memory on essential details was accurate was her statement that she cut the cord long on the Tralee baby. Since the cord was, in fact, an unusually long one, this detail was perceived to be too much of a coincidence to be other than factual.

Bridie Fuller never said that she cut the cord long.

She was told that she did.

She was told by her own lawyer, and then by the judge, in the following verbatim exchange.

McCarthy: You haven't been a maternity nurse but the baby's body showed something over a foot of umbilical cord attached to the body?

Justice Lynch: No, I think it was about six inches.

McCarthy: Thirty-six centimetres.

Justice Lynch: Not thirty-six inches.

McCarthy: A very long length of umbilical cord, thirty-six centimetres, which is over a foot?

BF: Yes.

McCarthy: When you cut the cord, you left a great deal of umbilical cord on the body?

BF: Yes.

McCarthy then moved on to another topic. The judge interrupted him after a few moments to address Bridie Fuller directly: 'It is correct to say it was fourteen and a half inches, or thirty-six centimetres. I was momentarily confused that it was six to eight inches that Dr Harbison said you cut it. Sorry for interrupting. It seemed to be confusing in the background.'

Since Dr Harbison had never stated that Bridie cut anything, the police lawyers attempted to sort out the judge's continuing confusion. Their case depended on the Cahirciveen 'twin' being born in Joanne's room and the Cahirciveen baby's cord had been sheared off at the navel. Bridie was questioned further.

Martin Kennedy: I don't understand about these things. Was it because the baby was weak that you cut the cord long? What has that got to do with it?

BF: I don't know, but the baby was weak.

MK: What effect would it have? Was it easier on the baby to cut the cord long?

BF: It was.

MK: Why?

BF: I don't know why.

Anthony Kennedy: Would I be right in thinking that maybe you would cut it in the normal sort of way somewhere near the body?

BF: Really, he was so very chesty and everything that is probably why I had it longer than usual.

AK: Would I be right in thinking that apart from cutting it, you didn't pay much attention as to where you cut it?

BF: Yes.

AK: I am wondering whether you can think again about the question of the old cord . . . the first knot you would make would be as near to the baby as you could?

BF: Yes.

Judge: She said in her own words the child was chesty and that is why I cut the cord long. She is not to be trapped into saying yes or no . . . The evidence impresses me . . .

The judge did not intervene when Bridie Fuller answered yes and no to his own senior counsel.

Mr Moriarty to Ms Fuller: Can you tell us how much assistance you were able to give . . . was there any question of breaking the waters?

BF: No.

Moriarty: You are saying you didn't break the waters?

BF: No.

Mr Moriarty later secured the statement which Bridie Fuller had made to the police and he quoted an extract to her.

Moriarty: '. . . Joanne was at an advanced stage. We went up to see her and I helped break her waters.' Did you say that?

BF: That is right.

Moriarty: The bit that you mentioned about breaking the waters, can you remember now whether or not you did break the waters or not?

BF: Yes.

Moriarty: Whereas two days ago I think you said you may not have helped to break the waters?

BF: Yes.

Moriarty: Can you remember whether you did or not?

BF: I remember now.

Moriarty: You remember what about the waters?

BF: Yes.

Moriarty: That you did help in breaking them?

BF: Yes.

Martin Kennedy: Had the waters burst when you first saw Joanne?

BF: They had, I suppose.

The sick old woman in the wheelchair was even more contradictory on the washing of the baby.

McCarthy: You didn't wash the baby?

BF: No.

McCarthy: So far as you are concerned nobody washed the baby?

BF: No.

Anthony Kennedy: As a nurse yourself . . . and a great nurse, you would be very anxious to have everything as clean as possible?

BF: Yes.

AK: Would I be right in thinking that you would clean off as much as you could?

BF: Yes.

AK: And Kathleen gave you all the water you wanted?

BF: Yes.

AK: So that you would clean its face and its body and every bit of it you could get at?

BF: Yes.

AK: And then get at some of the awkward places like under its armpits, to give it a bit of a wipe down?

BF: Yes.

AK: You would clean its eyes to see. We know a child can't see but you would give it a chance to open its eyes?

BF: Yes.

AK: And it is a good idea to try and get it out of the ears?

BF: Yes.

AK: Do you remember doing that, cleaning it up?

BF: I do.

AK: It would be important to clean it up down near its genitals?

BF: Yes.

AK: Did you give it a good sort of rub down and wiped and washed it in all these places?

BF: I did.

AK: You made it as spick and span as you could?

BF: The child was very chesty and I think I cleaned it up all right.

McCarthy: Was there any reason why it wasn't washed?

BF: Because it was very chesty.

Evidence had already been given to the tribunal that the body of Joanne Hayes's baby had not been washed after the birth. Bridie Fuller had the following to say about whether or not Joanne Hayes was pregnant at all.

Moriarty: Can you say how long before she had the baby that you would have suspected that she was pregnant?

BF: I did not suspect really.

Moriarty: From the way she looked did she seem to be getting bigger?

BF: She did, really.

Moriarty: Can you say how long before the birth that would have been?

BF: About a month before it.

Moriarty: The evidence will be, if it refreshes your memory . . . that the first few detectives who spoke to you asked you about Joanne being pregnant. Do you remember?

BF: Yes.

Moriarty: What did you state to them early on in the day, do you remember?

BF: I can't remember.

Moriarty: Again the evidence will be that early on in the day when the detectives asked you about Joanne being pregnant you said, first of all, you didn't know she was pregnant.

BF: I did not know she was pregnant.

Moriarty: From the evidence you gave us two days ago it seems that you would have known from being present in the house. Is that right?

BF: Yes.

Moriarty: Can you say why it was you maybe didn't tell the full story of things first of all?

BF: Well, I thought she wasn't pregnant.

Moriarty: But you told us two days ago that you had been in the house when the various things you describe took place?

BF: Yes.

Moriarty: What I'm asking you is maybe why the first time the guards asked you some questions did you say she wasn't pregnant?

BF: I thought she wasn't pregnant.

Judge: She is, I think, drawing a distinction between that night and earlier on. Some time before she did not know she was pregnant.

The split-second distinction between knowing and not knowing would have done credit to a Jesuit, and Mr Moriarty accepted it.

Moriarty: Yes, in fact the position is you didn't know at an early stage she was pregnant?

BF: Yes.

AK: I know nothing about when a baby is born, being a man. You, a nurse, would know all about it maybe?

BF: I wouldn't because I did not do maternity.

After hearing Bridie Fuller the lawyers returned to court where counsel for the judge, Mr Duggan, said: 'She was very lucid. She was very relaxed and was perfectly clear about what she was saying. Not alone that but the doctor gave absolute clearance for her.' Counsel for the Attorney General, Mr O'Higgins, said: 'We know she is not ga-ga and we know she is in the full use of her reason because the doctors told us and we could see it with our own eyes . . . the judge heard her and said she was very helpful.'

The judge's senior counsel, Mr Moriarty, said that her evidence showed 'apparent clarity in many respects'.

Bridie's sister greeted these sentiments with the exasperated snort that Bridie hadn't 'got her wits about her at all' and had been mentally disabled for years. The incensed judge immediately ordered doctors into court to contradict what Mr Moriarty described as 'certain remarks made by Miss Joan Fuller and reported widely in the press and television in relation to the capacity of Miss Bridie Fuller to give evidence'.

Dr McEneaney was asked if Bridie was 'a fully competent witness?' She was, he said.

The judge was not satisfied, and he took up questioning himself. 'We had a lady down here yesterday from Newbridge and she said her sister Bridie, whom she had not seen since Christmas, was getting more feeble-minded every day and is not responsible for what she is saying. Is there any basis in truth for that?'

'Not that I am aware of,' said Dr McEneaney.

Dr Chute was then called. On 3 January he had told the Hayes solicitor that he was not qualified to say whether Bridie Fuller was fit or not. On 30 January, when Dr McEneaney declared the woman unfit, Mr Anthony Kennedy alleged that Dr Chute had refused to come to a similar finding. On 2 February Dr Chute had his solicitors write to the papers to contradict Mr Kennedy, stating that 'our client has never been and is not now Ms Fuller's medical attendant . . . the question of his refusal to certify that Ms Fuller was unfit to give evidence does not arise'. On 7 February, the day after Dr McEneaney revised his findings to declare Bridie Fuller capable, Dr Chute came into court to revise his.

He had formed the opinion on 3 January, he told the court, that Bridie Fuller was 'fit to attend', adding, 'I hadn't medically examined her.'

Undeterred by this oversight, Justice Lynch said, 'Your opinion is she was fit to attend at that time on 3 January?'

Dr Chute replied, 'Yes.'

Such revision, by such experts, was to plague the tribunal. Months later psychiatrist John Fennelly, on instructions from the tribunal, examined Bridie Fuller and pronounced her senile, 'deteriorated and deteriorating still'. He regarded her memory as 'probably more inaccurate than unreliable'.

Bridie Fuller's testimony, then as now, haunted the public imagination. What had she seen through that long night by the range, as Joanne came through the kitchen in a blood-stained nightie?

II

Mary Hayes also revised her testimony. The revolving-door method of the tribunal meant that she spoke, Bridie spoke, Joan Fuller spoke, then she spoke, then Bridie spoke, then she spoke. Mary Hayes told the tribunal at first that she had not been present at all on the night of 12/13 April. Kathleen, Ned and Mike were mistaken in thinking they had said goodnight to her in the kitchen. She had watched television with Joanne and gone to bed early. She had slept from ten o'clock right through to ten the following morning.

The lawyers reminded her that her sister Bridie had subsequently said otherwise and Mary Hayes then yielded up the details of a night to which she had closed her eyes, changing those details as they pressed her for exact recall, each man cross-checking what she had told the other. She had not been in bed but in the kitchen; no she had been on her way to bed, between the kitchen and the bedroom, when Joanne went outside; no she had been in bed when Joanne went outside.

Finally she said that she had just gone to bed in Mike's room, which is the middle one of the three bedrooms, when Joanne got up. Joanne had to come down the corridor, past Mike's room and then Bridie's room to go into the kitchen, where the front door gave directly onto the garden path. She heard her daughter come down the corridor and go out of the kitchen into the night.

After a while Mary Hayes called out to Kathleen that she should see what was keeping Joanne. She heard Kathleen open the kitchen door, heard her call 'Are you all right?', did not hear the reply, and heard Joanne come in some time later.

When Joanne finally came back down the corridor to go to bed, she paused at the open door of Mike's bedroom and said in response to her mother that she was all right. It was dark, said Mary Hayes, and from her bed she could not see.

Next morning she saw the blood on the kitchen floor and Joanne told her that she had had a heavy period. While Joanne was in hospital, Aquinas confirmed that it was a miscarriage.

Had she changed her testimony, the judge asked her, because she was anxious to place the birth in the field?

'You are a religious and pious woman,' Anthony Kennedy

addressed her. 'Should you by any chance commit perjury and die on the spot . . . do you not believe that you would be condemned for eternity, having died after committing a mortal sin. You believe that as part of your religion? You have taken an oath to have God come down and witness what you say is true and if you then swore false, it is eternal damnation and perdition. And in the teeth of that warning are you sticking to your story? There is not one ounce of truth in what Bridie Fuller was saying?'

Kevin O'Higgins read out to her the oath that James Duggan had read out to her son Mike. Was she calling both her son and her sister perjurers? Was she in bed or in the kitchen on that night? 'I am going to press you on it. I'm going to stay here as long as necessary until you answer that question.'

'I was between the bed and the kitchen,' she said. The birth hung between the house and the field.

Joan Fuller couldn't enlighten them. Surely, she said, it was secretly done, in the field. A Christian family would have helped had they known. Her family had never discussed the birth in detail. It was not necessary. They were Christians. She stumbled and slipped as she left the witness box. She and Mary Hayes left the court and wandered arm-in-arm with an Abbeydorney neighbour out onto the concrete platform that flanked the steps. There was a sheer ten-foot drop to the street. As they walked blindly forward, Detective Sergeant Gerry O'Carroll called frantically to them to step back, step back from the edge.

In Abbeydorney a woman got up in the middle of the night, sleepless, and hung her washing out in the dark.

22. Cords

The fourteen-and-a-half-inch umbilical cord that was found on Joanne Hayes's dead baby strangled the million-pound six-month enquiry from beginning to end. There was as much evidence assembled around it as was gathered around the deaths of Pope John Paul I and President Kennedy, and still the questions remain unanswered. Who killed Kennedy? How was the baby's cord severed?

Like the ancient mariner, Justice Kevin Lynch carried the cord wherever he went, from Tralee to Dublin, through all the seasons, asking of all and sundry and the most unlikely – Sister Aquinas – how the severing of the cord had come to pass. His most plaintive exchange took place with the elderly nun.

'How did the umbilical cord get cut if the baby was born outside? . . . Have you ever found out who cut the cord? . . . Assuming I find that the baby was born in the field, how was the umbilical cord cut? . . . Would it be possible for a mother to break an umbilical cord? . . . Would it be possible for a person – when I say a person, I mean the mother – to break an umbilical cord which I assume to be very greasy and slippery?'

She was gentle with him and with the chorus of men who echoed him. She did not know what a mother was capable of. All she knew was what Bridie was capable of. 'Bridie was not a maternity nurse. I doubt if she ever cut a cord in her life.' She told them fondly of the time when Bridie, on night duty at the hospital, was asked by the ambulance men to come and attend to a woman who had given birth in a field.

149

Bridie absolutely refused to go to the field unless a maternity nurse came along.

Long before Bridie or Aquinas or Joanne Hayes herself had taken the stand, in the opening week of the inquiry in fact, the state pathologist, John Harbison, had declared that the cord on Joanne's baby 'appeared' to have been cut with an implement. Joanne Hayes, fully aware of his statement, said again and again that she had broken the cord with her hands.

The conflict between the mother and the expert gave rise to much speculation. If the expert was right, why would Joanne Hayes tell a lie? Was she afraid to admit to premeditation – to going deliberately into a field with scissors that she would use to part herself from a baby which she then intended to abandon? Was she afraid that, if she admitted to scissors, the tribunal might make a connection between scissors and the stabbed Cahirciveen baby and seriously consider that she had indeed had twins? Was she protecting some other member of the family who had helped her deliver in the field, or all the members of the family who had helped her deliver in the farmhouse?

Or was she in fact telling the truth, and was the expert wrong?

The men of the tribunal and the succession of male experts who were called in to help pitted their wits, their implements and their experience against each other on the question of the cord. On two occasions it emerged that one simple test could prove decisively whether it had been severed by an instrument or pulled part by bare hands. 'The telling factor,' said Professor Robert Harrison, lecturer and consultant in gynaecology, would be a microscopic examination of 'the blood vessels, because they are rigid'. The outer flesh of the cord might be soft and its appearance misleading after severance, but the three minute veins which the flesh enclosed, pumping blood from the mother's womb to the baby's heart, lungs and kidneys, were strung with continuous, rigid blood vessels, whose appearance when severed would not mislead. Mr John Creedon agreed with him.

When the state pathologist was subsequently recalled to the witness stand, where he repeated that in his opinion the flesh had been cut through with an implement, he did not mention the blood vessels, nor was he asked about them. Long after the tribunal ended he acknowledged that he had not done that test. Had this been a murder trial, he explained, he would have examined the blood vessels in order to remove all possible doubt, but this was only an inquiry.

The judge brought his own unique testing methods to bear. He had acquired a reputation for accuracy and grasp of detail during his long years in commercial and civil litigation, and his reputation survived such blunders as announcing during Bridie Fuller's testimony that the by now fabled fourteen-and-a-half-inch umbilical cord was a precise six inches long, and insisting, much later, that the Cahirciveen baby's umbilical cord had been tied with thread, though it had been sheared off flush with the navel.

The judge used a pocket calculator, a magnifying glass and a piece of string to help him come to a decision about the cord. He was precise to the point of obsession about exactitude, insisting that the tribunal even estimate the length of that part of the cord which was missing. To this end, Sergeant Coughlan was made to describe a piece of material found in the field, which Kathleen had pointed out to him. It could have been either the afterbirth or the remains of the cord. It could have been something else entirely. Forensic scientists had been unable to determine whether this material was animal or human.

But supposing it were human, and supposing it were the cord, the judge wanted to know – what length was it? It was about two and a half to three feet in length, the sergeant said. 'How does it compare with the width of that witness box which is three feet four inches?' the judge asked. The sergeant was given a piece of string, asked to select that length of it which approximated to the length of the remains which he had found and instructed to place the selected length of string along the edge of the box, while the judge and his team of lawyers made visual calculations.

The sergeant opted for the full width of the box, and then again for slightly less.

The tribunal's junior, Mr Duggan, embarked on the mathematical elucidation. Professor Harrison, he said, had pronounced the average umbilical cord to be approximately three foot four. Mr Creedon had opted for around three feet. If one added the known length of the cord on the Tralee baby, fourteen and a half inches, to what, for the sake of argument, might be considered the remains of the cord, which the sergeant estimated to be on his biggest measurement four foot two and a half inches, and 'on your smallest measurement, three foot eight and a half inches', that would give either a five-foot-five-inch cord, or a three-foot-eleven-inch cord.

'That,' said Mr Duggan, 'would make it more than the average length as given?' Supercord!

Unless, the judge mused later, 'you are dealing with two cords. If that is so . . .' Take one cord from the room, marry it with the cord in the field and hey presto! Twins!

The tribunal considered whether a woman could, in any case, tear a cord apart. Almost impossible, given the cord's tensile strength, said Dr Harbison. 'It would be difficult,' doubted Professor Harrison, 'unless you stood on one end and pulled.' A woman could 'just about' do it, said Mr Creedon, though it would slip out of her hands, unless she had rough gloves on.

Would the cord be long enough, asked the judge, to wrap around each hand, taking for example the fourteen-and-a-half-inch part and 'presumably a bit more to the placenta?' Mr Creedon said he remembered the exact same question from the judge on his previous occasion in the witness box, 'and I felt like going and trying it. I have not.'

He could still do so, he offered.

There was no need. The state pathologist had been tearing cords apart in anticipation of a recall. He announced during the closing stage of the tribunal that it could indeed be done. He had also invited women students to engage in the trial of strength. Were the women able to do it? Easily. Not only that, but the lightest of the students, at seven and a half stone, lighter even than Joanne Hayes, was the strongest. 'So much for the guidelines of what a small female can pull,' he said.

Dr Declan Gilsenan, who acts as state pathologist when Dr Harbison is unavailable, had also been experimenting with umbilical cords. He queried his colleague's assertion that the cord had been cut. He had spent a weekend cutting cords up, with both a knife and scissors. The knife 'invariably cuts the cord straight across, perhaps slightly raggedly.' The photograph of the Tralee baby's cord showed such a straight cut. However, that cut had been made by Dr Harbison when slicing off a piece of the cord for examination.

The other end of the sample, showing the break presumably made by Joanne Hayes, was clearly diagonal. One could not make a diagonal cut by simply snipping a cord that floated freely between a woman and her baby. To achieve that diagonal cut one would have to deliberately place the cord on a hard surface and then cut through, said Dr Gilsenan. This he had done, repeatedly, in order to be sure of his conclusions.

Judge Lynch lent Mr Creedon his magnifying glass that he might study the photo of the cord. 'It does not look like a cut end, does it, my lord? I don't think it looks like a cut end.'

Justice Lynch: Dr Harbison said it appeared to have been cut, on microscopic examination.

Creedon: Under microscopy he should be able to tell if the vessels are severed or broken.

The men delved ever deeper into the mystery. If Bridie Fuller had indeed cut the cord and tied it with cotton thread to prevent blood loss, should not the piece of thread still be on the cord? There was no knotted thread on the cord, nor indeed the slightest indentation on the flesh to suggest that a knot had ever been there. The judge again lent Mr Creedon his magnifying glass, that both men might double-check the findings of the state pathologist.

Young Mr Duggan put forward a theory. 'Are you familiar, Mr Creedon, with the way they castrate young bulls?' He explained that a winching device was affixed to the bull's testicles and left in place for a few days, during which time the winch gradually cut through, until both winch and that which it was supposed to sever fell right off.

'A live bull?' winced Mr Creedon.

'A live young bull. It is the constant pressure,' explained Mr Duggan. Might not the thread have similarly tightened on the umbilical cord of Joanne Hayes's baby until it cut right through? There would not have been time, Mr Duggan was reminded. The baby had died almost instantly, and was placed within hours in a bag. Even if the thread had cut through, both it and the severed remains would have been found in the bag.

In any case, the state pathologist, John Harbison, had concluded that the cord was cut after death.

'After death?' the judge asked.

'After death,' Mr Harbison repeated.

The possibility existed that Joanne Hayes had been telling the truth. That she had given birth in the field, panicked and put her hand over the baby's mouth, killing it instantly. That she had then separated herself from her dead son by tearing the cord that bound them together. The tribunal never asked her to give specific details of the manner of that dreadful separation. Detail was the preserve of the experts. And Bridie Fuller.

Joanne Hayes was only the mother.

23. Twins

The tribunal turned its attention to the possibility that Joanne Hayes might have had twins. Doubtful though they were that a woman could be strong enough to tear an umbilical cord apart with her bare hands, the men devoted serious attention to the possibility that this woman had been strong enough to deliver herself of a baby in a field, go in home and be delivered within the hour by Bridie Fuller of another, which she then stabbed in panic, and manage all the while to stay calmly secretive about the first. Should the police discover the corpse of the second twin, which Joanne Hayes instructed her brothers to bury at sea, and should the rest of the family subsequently sing like frightened canaries about that child, this woman would produce a small but perfectly formed alibi – the baby in the field.

Diabolically clever!

But then, as one psychiatrist told the tribunal, he had once treated a woman who not only claimed to have had sexual intercourse with the devil, but persuaded her family of the fact.

Diabolical!

And then again, learned men sitting on tribunals long before this one, Catholic holy men at that, had found that the women brought before them did indeed have sexual intercourse with the devil. The devil, found these holy men, had a penis that was cold as ice. The women they convicted were burned to death.

Diabolical!

Martin Kennedy put the case succinctly for the superintendents, who claimed that Joanne Hayes had conceived twins by two different men, each of whom had different blood groups. 'Is it possible,' he asked the experts, 'and it is the kernel of this tribunal, that a man may have intercourse with a woman and deposit semen in her vagina, and within ninety-six hours another man might have intercourse with the same woman and deposit semen in her vagina, is it possible if that happened . . . that a woman could be impregnated in one ovum from the semen of the first one and in another ovum from the semen of the second man?'

'Or in the same ovum?' added the judge.

It was a very rare possibility. He had heard about it in conversation, said Dr Harbison.

The conversation about Joanne Hayes went on in public and in private for months. There was open speculation about the kind of woman she was. In a national daily newspaper a journalist declared that she did not have the kind of personality that would attract him. 'Probably a matter of chemistry,' he wrote. Another journalist who had never met her wrote that he had heard that she was 'a cheeky strap'.

While they waited for the real expert to arrive from England and pronounce upon the possibility of superfecundation, the tribunal tried to establish whether Joanne Hayes had carried twins by debating the way she had looked while pregnant in 1984.

Her workmate, a nurse, testified that she had looked as though she were only carrying one baby. Anthony Kennedy objected that the evidence of 'a mere nurse' could not be accepted. (He had not yet made the acquaintance of Bridie Fuller, whom he described as 'a great nurse'.)

Detective Smith recalled receiving a visit at home from a man who lived up his road. This was after Joanne Hayes had been charged with killing the Cahirciveen baby. They both heard the radio newsflash about the finding of her Tralee baby. The visiting electrician had immediately solved the conundrum. 'My God, she has had twins; the size of her! She was huge.'

Tralee gynaecologist John Creedon was invited by the judge to speculate on Joanne Hayes's probable appearance had she been carrying both the Tralee baby and the Cahirciveen baby. First they considered her normal appearance.

Mr Creedon: She is one metre forty-four centimetres tall. That's four foot eight and a half inches.

Judge: Four foot eight and three-quarters. I am sure we will not quarrel with a quarter of an inch.

Mr Creedon: And weighs forty-six kilos and 300 grammes. Approximately seven stone.

Judge: And three and three-quarter pounds.

Add twins of 5.26 pounds and 6 pounds, total 11.62 pounds, plus three pound for two placentas, Mr Creedon calculated aloud. The court waited while he thought. 'She would certainly have looked very large indeed. She would be grossly distended. She would have to compensate by leaning back and her attitude would be very military. Her spine would be extended backwards in order to maintain her sphere of gravity. It would not have been possible to miss noticing.'

Professor Robert Harrison dismissed Mr Creedon's painstaking calculations as speculation. It was not possible to tell by looking at a woman's size that she was expecting twins. As for posture and military bearing, 'some women are earth-mother types, who strut and waddle, others retain their femininity'.

Abandoning this method of deciding whether or not Joanne Hayes had had twins – by anybody – and still waiting, as the months went by, for the superfecundation expert to arrive from England, the tribunal considered whether super-fecundation was the key at all. Supposing Joanne Hayes had had twins by Jeremiah Locke, both parents blood-group O, and both babies blood-group O? All the tribunal had to establish was that the Cahirciveen baby was never blood-group A in the first place. Dr Gilsenan was brought along to prove this. (Before dealing with the blood, he dealt with the baby's wounds. His tests had shown that the knife found in the Hayes household could have caused them, although Dr Harbison's tests had shown that the knife could not have done so.)

Dr Gilsenan suggested that a sample of the Cahirciveen baby's lung tissue, which had been used for blood-grouping purposes, was contaminated. Therefore the A-grouping could be wrong. He had not examined this sample for contamination, mind you. He had examined another sample altogether, from the baby's other lung, 'and it would be most unreasonable to assume the contamination in one could be different to that in the other'.

After Dr Gilsenan, an expert from England flew in to say that contamination could not change blood-group A to blood-group O. However, immersion could. So yet another expert was flown in to say he had done blood tests on two halves of the same female corpse, each half pulled out of the Thames at two different times. The top half gave one blood group reading, the bottom half gave a different one entirely.

The only way you could be sure with any sample, said this expert, was to do repeated tests. The woman who had originally identified the Cahirciveen baby as group A, Dr Louise McKenna, was recalled to the tribunal. She announced that she had done four tests and then asked the paternity tester of Northern Ireland to check her results. The paternity tester was brought down from Belfast to affirm this and the English expert flew home. The Cahirciveen baby was blood-group A.

This left them with a superfecundation situation.

While awaiting the superfecundation expert the police lawyers filled in the time with evidence culled from research of their own. Martin Kennedy had been furnished with data from a German doctor who claimed to have established that out of ten thousand sets of twins born in his hospital, one hundred sets had been conceived by two different fathers. An incidence of one per cent! 'If he means that he finds that sort of incidence of superfecundation in his hospital, it surprises me,' said Professor Harrison. 'Is it published?'

'I asked him that,' said Mr Kennedy, 'and he said nobody wants to know.' Anthony Kennedy was relying on a published work called *Williams on Obstetrics*. 'Would you accept,' he asked Mr Creedon, 'that *Williams on Obstetrics* is an absolutely standard work?'

'I don't know that one,' said Mr Creedon.

'It is,' said Mr Kennedy, 'a recognised authoritative work. It is the garda síochána [police] guide for everyday problems to be solved, by instant reference to that authority. Have you never heard of it? Can it be true you never heard of *Williams on Obstetrics*?' Mr Creedon had not. Professor Robert Harrison had: 'It is a post-graduate textbook. It is not important.'

Mr Kennedy produced a cutting from the *Daily Mirror*, which he wanted Professor Harrison to consider. 'Unfortunately' it did not have a page-three picture, said Mr Kennedy, to the guffaws of his colleagues. What it did have was a story on a West German half-caste woman who had had twins, one black and one white. She claimed that the twins were conceived of two men, one a white German, the other a black American soldier. This, said Mr Anthony Kennedy, was evidence of superfecundation.

That, said the professor, was a 1978 publication based on a 1962 event. The *Daily Mirror* was late with its news. The judge intervened to query the story. He did not question its veracity, merely the character of the woman concerned. 'What sort of ladies are we dealing with here?' For the first time in months, the men of the tribunal were brought to realise that they had been speculating on the character of Joanne Hayes when they bandied about stories of women who slept around.

Psychiatrists were brought in to give opinions on her character.

24. What Sort of Lady?

Detective Sergeant Dillon, who had brought the police from Cahirciveen to Tralee to investigate Joanne Hayes as a suspect for the murder of the Cahirciveen baby, had very definite ideas about her character. 'I knew her to salute going in and out of the sports centre. She was not a person that would return a salute, you know, and sometimes I would look for armbands for swimming and she always gave me the impression that I was disturbing her.'

After receiving her name from his hospital informant, he went to Abbeydorney to check her out: 'I was in an unmarked car with Detective Sergeant O'Donnell and we were driving past the Hayes home and I saw Joanne on a roadway wheeling her pram. She was definitely watching the car to see who was in it when we came along. As we were coming up to her, she was looking at the car to see who was in it and when we came face to face with her she put her eyes down to the ground.'

The tribunal heard many reasons why a woman couldn't look a man in the eye. 'These are things nobody wants to talk about,' Professor Harrison pointed out. In one English hospital alone it was found that twenty-one per cent of the men coming deludedly into the maternity ward to see their off-spring were not the fathers at all.

The professor, practising in Dublin's most famous maternity hospital, the Rotunda, no longer asked questions in front of prospective fathers. 'I wouldn't ask the woman in the presence of her husband and I wouldn't write the reply down.'

Although it was medically possible to disprove paternity, it

160

was impossible to prove it. 'You can never say somebody is the father.' That knowledge a woman could carry with her to the grave. No man can know. He can only trust.

Dr John Fennelly, chief psychiatrist in Limerick mental hospital, met Joanne Hayes in jail after Detective Dillon had arrested her and charged her with the murder of the Cahirciveen baby. He found her ill, depressed and suicidal and had her transferred immediately to his hospital. She insisted that she was not the mother of the Cahirciveen baby and recovered swiftly when her own baby was found. She spoke often and lovingly of Jeremiah Locke, the father of her dead child.

Martin Kennedy came straight to the point. 'Did she love this man or love what this man or some other man was prepared to do with her?' Pursuing his thesis on the sort of lady the tribunal was dealing with, to paraphrase the judge, Mr Kennedy explained that if he could show that Joanne Hayes was 'interested in sexual activity for its own sake, and not for the sake of loving a particular man', he would be well on the road to establishing superfecundation. All he had to establish was that it was more than likely that, while Joanne Hayes was 'carrying on' with Jeremiah Locke, she was also 'carrying on' with another man.

'Carrying on is a euphemism for having sex.' He abandoned delicacy.

The judge allowed him to pursue his thesis.

Dr Fennelly believed that she loved Jeremiah Locke. She worried that he was 'having a rough time of it' since her arrest. She was afraid that Yvonne would now be taken from her. She worried about her mother, whom she had never told of her third pregnancy and who had now learned about it in the most horrible way.

She described how she had panicked during the birth in the field and said she killed the baby by putting her hands over its mouth 'after it cried'. The psychiatrist felt that at all times Joanne Hayes was truthful with him.

Anthony Kennedy hailed the intelligence of the child's cry before death as 'a magnificent development'. It proved that the baby had achieved a separate existence. It proved that the mother was a killer. It proved that the police were right to charge her with killing some baby, any baby, details to be sorted out later. The baby had briefly lived and the baby had swiftly died.

Magnificent.

He sketched a picture of the sort of lady they had here, and the psychiatrist agreed with the police lawyer's outline. He agreed that a woman who kept silent about birth, 'through thick and thin', who did not discuss it even with her family, was clearly a person of 'persistent and resilient make-up', 'cute', 'of a cunning and scheming nature' and a 'fairly devious turn of mind'.

He agreed that mental disturbance at the time of birth in a perfectly stable woman was quite common, even if the child-birth were uneventful, and agreed that until her hormonal level adjusted itself a woman would be in 'a tricky mental state'.

Still and all, Dr Fennelly said he would give Joanne Hayes the benefit of the doubt that she had not tried to kill her baby. There would not have been, he thought, premeditation.

The psychiatrist was asked to examine Joanne Hayes once more to see how she was, nearly one year after the birth and death of her son in April 1984. He returned to the tribunal to tell them that the sort of lady they had here now, in March 1985, was bright and cheerful and did not appear to be upset. She did not have a great degree of guilt at this stage. 'Not as much perhaps as I would have thought she would.' He did not say just how much guilt he felt a woman ought to have.

She was, he agreed with Anthony Kennedy, narcissistic. He did not think she was frigid. She was a sociopath with a histri-onic personality. The two men went through the fourteen-point guideline to a histrionic personality and agreed that all the points fitted Joanne Hayes. She exhibited:

1. superficial charm and average or superior intelligence
2. absence of irrationality – at ease in situations which would unsettle the average individual
3. no sense of responsibility
4. no sense of shame
5. a cavalier attitude to telling the truth
6. anti-social behaviour with no apparent regret
7. poor judgement and regular failure to learn from experience
8. lack of genuine insight
9. callousness, insincerity and incapacity for love and attachment
10. little response to special consideration and kindness
11. no history of genuine suicide attempts
12. an unrestrained and unconventional sex life
13. failure to have a life plan, except to follow a consistent pattern of self-defeat
14. the onset of sociopathic characteristics occurring no later than the early 20s

On the other hand, Dr Fennelly pointed out, he had based this assessment partly on what he had read about Joanne Hayes in the papers, and anyway half the population of Ireland fitted that description.

Dr Brian McCaffrey, a psychiatrist who had never met or spoken with Joanne Hayes in his life, was called to comment upon her and upon Dr Fennelly's assessment of her. He, too, was relying on newspapers and notes, though he had watched her watching Dr Fennelly in court.

He had figured out that she was not suicidal the night Dr Fennelly met her in jail. He disagreed that she must have been depressed, though she must have felt genuine misery, and what's more he felt that she was the best example of the princess-victim syndrome he had ever encountered. She was a victim of the tribunal and princess of the media.

The two psychiatrists were agreed on one thing only. Both men felt that Joanne Hayes had not purged herself sufficiently to satisfy their standards of normal behaviour for a woman. She had been imprisoned and lodged in a mental home, had cried her heart out before the tribunal, had hyperventilated and vomited, had been sedated and brought back for more, but, said Dr Fennelly, there was 'not a great degree of guilt at this stage, not as much as I might have thought she would have'.

She didn't look right, at a distance, to Dr McCaffrey either: 'It didn't have the impact on her that it would have on a normal individual.'

Anthony Kennedy suggested that she was 'actually taking pleasure in her great struggle with the law and even taking pride in her accomplishment in winning, as she'd see it'.

Even, added the judge, 'taking pleasure in the whole hub-bub that we're all engaged in?' Overall, agreed Dr Fennelly, 'the tribunal hasn't had a deleterious effect on her'.

'Which has to be abnormal in some way; to thrive on it,' said Mr Kennedy. It was perfectly normal of course, for the men to thrive on it; to pore over pictures of dead babies before adjourning to a hearty lunch; to pose specially for the television cameras, any television cameras, after the public had gone home and the day's speculation on Joanne Hayes's private life been done with; to make sure the journalists got exactly right every word that issued from their mouths.

That was quite normal.

Anyway, said Dr McCaffrey, clinical director of psychiatry for the Eastern Health Board, Joanne Hayes had 'got herself pregnant on three occasions'. The tribunal, now nearing the end of its six-month existence, accepted without demur the notion that a woman could impregnate herself at will. It would do in the absence of the superfecundation expert, of whom there was still no sign.

25. Love is for Life

While the tribunal conducted its trial of womanhood, from January to June, the Catholic Church engaged in a trial of strength with the government over the right to control women's fertility. Side by side with the headlines about Joanne Hayes ran headlines about the battle between Church and state over contraception. The media talked about the biggest, most grave confrontation between the two institutions since the foundation of the Republic.

The minister for health wanted to make condoms available, without prescription, to all adults over the age of eighteen. Pharmacists, he stressed, need not sell them if their consciences forbade them.

Kevin McNamara, whose promotion from bishop of Kerry to archbishop of Dublin had been televised as he sat on a throne in the Pro-Cathedral while women danced before him on the altar, declared that the proposal to sell condoms placed Irish society 'at a decisive moral crossroads'. He warned that 'the bitter fruits' of such a policy would be 'moral decline, the growth of venereal disease, and a sharp increase in the number of teenage pregnancies, illegitimate births and abortions'. He reminded Catholics of the existence of hell and asked how any doctor or health-board official claiming to be Christian could say 'I am prepared, if the state so decides, to supply to those who ask, the means which will help them to commit serious sin?'

Seventeen of the country's most powerful senior consultants and doctors warned that the liberalisation of contraceptive laws would lead to 'an increase in promiscuity with an upsurge in venereal diseases and carcinoma of the cervix', in a letter to the government. Two of these men, Professor John Bonnar and Professor Eamon de Valera, had previously been prominent in the anti-abortion campaign.

All the priests in Kerry signed a statement, read out at all Masses, that 'artificial contraception and premarital sexual intercourse are always wrong'. The Kerry Diocesan Council for the Family, a lay organisation, said that there was no need, nor demand, for change in the laws.

The bishop of Limerick said that the proposed legislation was not acceptable on the grounds of public morality, 'whether or not the majority of the people might think otherwise'.

Charles Haughey declared his party's total opposition to the notion of contraception for any but married couples. Several members of the governing coalition fled their homes, declaring that their lives were under threat, three defied the government whip posing the threat of a general election, the corpse of a new-born infant was found in Galway railway station, the statue of the Virgin Mary was seen to move in a Kerry church, attracting a weekly sightseeing throng of thousands, and the sale of condoms without prescription was legalised by a narrow majority in Dáil Éireann on 14 February.

In Tralee, eleven of the twelve pharmacies continued their refusal to stock them.

In March all the catholic bishops of Ireland met in conference and issued a pastoral on love, sexuality and the family, entitled *Love is for Life*. The bishops defined the meaning of sex. Sexual union, wrote the bishops, was the means by which a man and a woman said to each other:

> I love you. There is nobody else in all the world I love in the way I love you. I love you just for being you. I want you to become even more wonderful than you are. I want to share my life and my world with you. I want you to share your life and your world with me. I want us to build a new

> life together, a future together, which will be our future. I
> need you. I can't live without you. I need you to love me,
> and to love me not just now but always. I will be faithful to
> you not just now but always. I will never let you down or
> walk out on you. I will never put anyone else in place of
> you. I will stay with you through thick and thin. I will be
> responsible for you and I want you to be responsible for me,
> for us, no matter what happens.

The pastoral then spelt out the ground rules for achieving this saccharine state of purple bliss. Premarital and extramarital sex was out; so was cohabitation. God's mercy was there for those unmarried mothers 'who admit their sin and ask His pardon'. Contraception was out, as was sterilisation. If pregnancy resulted from rape, the 'right to life' of the unborn child 'must be respected'. Divorce was out.

The parish priests of Abbeydorney refused a request from the Hayes family to say Mass in their home.

Three days after the bishops had spoken, on 8 March, International Women's Day, the front page of the nation's evening newspaper was entirely taken up with stories about the female condition. An unmarried policewoman was under investigation by the force for behaviour prejudicial to it – she had had a baby. A judge had upheld the right of a Catholic school board to sack unmarried schoolteacher Eileen Flynn from her post – she had committed adultery and had a baby by the married man with whom she was living. The man had been separated for years from his wife, but divorce is illegal. A government deputy said that women should not be allowed to have jobs because the 'escalating social disorder' was due to the fact that 'married women are leaving the home to work'. Detective Sergeant Gerry O'Carroll told the Kerry babies tribunal that Joanne Hayes – from whom he had secured a confession of murder after interrogating her for eight hours – had probably had sexual intercourse with another man within forty-eight hours of having sexual intercourse with Jeremiah

Locke. 'Ireland is a promiscuous society and there are umpteen such cases,' he declared.

This particular case was only one such example, umpteen experts had pronounced upon it, it was about to draw to a close, and the announcement was made that the superfecundation expert was flying in on 9 May.

26. Tribunal Concludes

While awaiting the arrival of the superfecundation expert, the judge drew on his sporting background – he is a tennis enthusiast – to solve a couple of outstanding problems. How could the police have failed to locate the baby in the pool of water on the family farm? He ordered the police photographer to go out and do now that which the police had failed to do when Kathleen first brought them to the scene – take a picture of the area. He told the photographer to use a rugby ball to simulate a baby.

The photographer returned to tell the tribunal that the rugby ball refused to sink below the surface. He had filled the bag instead with clay and sods of grass.

The judge then asked the photographer to solve the second problem. Could, the judge asked, Joanne Hayes have really made her way to the pool by crossing a bedstead-cum-gate, given that she was 'four foot eight and three-quarter inches, weighing seven stones and nine pounds, carrying a parcel weighing about half a stone?' The photographer thought not.

The judge went out to the farm, accompanied by the media, to try for himself. He approached the gate head on, attempting the bars from ground level, and cleared it with some considerable difficulty. When a newspaper photograph subsequently appeared, showing Joanne avoiding the bars and using the more sensible method of stepping up on the ditch alongside to clear the reduced height like a gazelle, the judge returned to the farm. He did not invite the media along to watch his second outing.

When winter had turned to spring and the tribunal had moved from Tralee to Dublin and the superfecundation expert had still not arrived, the tribunal decided to kill time by dealing with anonymous letters that the judge had been receiving. These letters claimed that the mother of the Cahirciveen baby had been found dead and her death hushed up. The superintendent in charge of Kerry's police force was called to tell the tale of the Dutch woman who had hanged herself in the county around the time that Joanne Hayes was arrested.

The unprecedented revelation of a confidential suicide report was a measure of the lengths to which the tribunal was prepared, and forced, to go in order to bolster flagging public confidence. The Dutch woman, with a master's degree in Chinese culture, had been a leading member of the Campaign for Nuclear Disarmament in Amsterdam. A motorcycle accident left her mentally unstable. She tried to kill herself by lying on railway tracks in front of an oncoming train. The train cut one of her legs off. She came, crippled, from Holland to County Kerry and rented a house. She tried to emulate the life of a character in a popular Dutch work of fiction. This character, Momo, had withdrawn from a society corrupted by materialism.

The Dutch woman also withdrew and lived a vegetarian life in Kerry. Then she hanged herself. The autopsy showed that she was not pregnant nor recently delivered of a pregnancy. Her diaries showed no information about a love life. Besides, said the inspector, the landlord would have noticed if she were pregnant, he being a father of six.

The judge hoped that the woman's identity would be kept secret. The newspapers revealed her name. Once in a while it had to be shown that this tribunal came up with facts. Yet another expert had testified that the facts as believed in Ireland were anything but. For instance, said Dr Peter McCabe, the admiralty charts of Irish coastal waters were never within three hundred per cent of accuracy.

Dr McCabe had helped to build the Aswan dam in Egypt. He came to the tribunal to declare that Professor Peter Barry, an oceanographer from University College, Galway, who relied on those charts, was totally wrong to suggest that the Cahirciveen baby could not have floated from Slea Head to White Strand. Irish waters went clockwise round the island, true, and moved in that clockwise direction from White Strand up to Slea Head, true, and the police were claiming that the baby had floated anti-clockwise, from Slea Head down to White Strand, incredible, but the police were right. It was a matter of currents. He had no evidence to show that the currents went anti-clockwise from Slea Head to White Strand, he agreed.

Spring was showing hints of summer, and there were no rumours left to kill, when the superfecundation expert finally arrived at Dublin airport. The tribunal had a subpoena served on him to make sure that he would testify, regardless of his findings. He was a witness for the police after all, and he had not yet tested Joanne Hayes's blood, and the police might choose not to call him if his findings were unfavourable to them, besides which the lawyer for the Hayes family had expressed reluctance at having her blood sample released to him.

The superfecundation expert said that the possibility that Joanne Hayes might have had twins by two different fathers was so rare that it could be ruled out.

'The bastard shot us down,' Martin Kennedy said afterwards. In June the six-month saga of sub-pornographic scenarios, which saw Joanne Hayes regularly coupled, in brutal graphic seamy sleazy detail, with unidentified men in numbers unknown, came to an end. 'There were times when we all thought she had twins,' said Judge Kevin Lynch.

As lawyers made their closing submissions, Marguerite Egan of the Tralee women's group stepped up to the judge's bench and placed a sealed envelope upon it. What was in the envelope, he asked her? A submission on behalf of the women of Ireland, she replied. The submission lay unopened between them as they faced each other. It recommended, among other things, the abolition of all-male tribunals.

The judge with all his legal powers faced the woman with the yellow flower in her lapel. He could jail her for contempt, he said. Then he told her to go away and have some sense. 'What,' he asked, 'have I got to do with the women of Ireland in general? What have the women of Ireland in general got to do with this case?'

27. A Woman to Blame

Bridie Fuller died in a geriatric home on 29 September 1985. She had been transferred directly there from the hospital in which she gave evidence. Her deteriorating condition required permanent medical supervision. She never recovered sufficiently to return home. The Hayes family visited her faithfully right up to the end, showing a palpable and unwavering affection that the events of the tribunal did not impair. Though they increasingly accepted that her testimony might damn and would certainly taint them for ever more, they mourned the loss of her, and the death of her, in tears, at her graveside.

Two days after she was buried, on 4 October, Judge Kevin Lynch released his report on the Kerry babies inquiry. He rained blow upon blow on the heads of the surviving members of the family. Joanne Hayes, he found, was not the mother of the Cahirciveen baby. But he exonerated the police from any major blame in charging her with its murder. She and her mother, her sister and her brothers were 'barefaced liars' who had misled the police and perjured themselves before him in an attempt to cover up the death of Joanne's baby. He did not answer clearly the central question and reason for the setting up of the tribunal – how did a family come to confess to a crime they could not have committed, and supply corroborative details known only to the police, and add imaginative details of their own?

The report stated that the family had in fact confessed to the police the true story of the death of their own baby 'with additions as to stabbing, and a journey, to fit involvement with the Cahirciveen baby'. Judge Lynch did not explain the source of those additions. He dismissed out of hand the explanations offered by the Hayeses. No member of the family was beaten. No member of the family was terrorised. By implication, though the judge does not spell out the incredible scenario, four members of the Hayes family – Joanne, Kathleen, Ned and Mike – seated in separate rooms in a police station, each spelled out the exact same fantasy, differing only in their estimation of the numbers present at and partaking in the fantasy. Joanne Hayes imagined, all by herself, that she stabbed the Cahirciveen baby to death, that the knife was brought to her by Kathleen, that she plunged the knife repeatedly into the baby and that Kathleen, Mike and Mary Hayes, plus Bridie Fuller, watched her do it.

Kathleen Hayes independently imagined that she carried the knife from the kitchen to the bedroom, placed it in Joanne's hands and watched Joanne plunge the knife into the infant. She also imagined that her mother, Mike and Bridie Fuller were present, that she and Ned and Mike had taken the corpse to Slea Head and that she had seen it float away.

Mike Hayes, a twenty-seven-year-old man with the intellectual and emotional development of a child, imagined and described in fluent detail how he, Kathleen and his mother and aunt had watched Joanne stab a baby to death, and how he and Ned had then driven the corpse away. Though he seldom in his life ventured off the farm, he managed to give clear details of the journey to the remote Dingle peninsula and was able to pinpoint a landmark bridge in Dingle town that guides the visitor wishing to go to Slea Head into the correct exit from a maze of exits. Ned Hayes imagined that he had taken a corpse from his sister's bedroom, that he and Mike had placed that corpse in a car and that they drove to Slea Head and threw the corpse into the water. He particularly imagined that they had shrouded the corpse in a specifically marked 0-7-30 fertiliser bag, an amazing coincidence, since the Cahirciveen baby's corpse was associated with just such a bag. The police were the only ones aware of that, and no such brand of fertiliser was ever used on the family farm. There was also the amazing coincidence, that only the police knew that the Cahirciveen baby was stabbed to death. The newspapers had not reported the nature of its wounds. It might have been kicked to death for all the public or the Hayes family knew, yet the Hayes family correctly fantasised a stabbing.

The report suggested that the fantastic confessions had resulted from a combination of the 'guilty conscience' of the Hayes family with 'pressure' from the police. It found no fault with police pressure. 'This was not a tea-party', the judge pointed out. The police had 'a strong suspicion that progressed into positive and certain belief' that they had on their hands a family which was lying about the death of some baby. The report does slap police wrists for an inadequate and cursory search of the farm after Joanne Hayes had supplied accurate details of the location of this dead baby, but invited sympathy for the police dilemma. Who could believe a story of birth in a field (three months after Anne Lovett)? Twenty-eight experienced police officers were up against a barefaced lying conspiracy, concocted by people who denied pregnancy, then admitted birth and death, then claimed not to know where the corpse was, then placed the corpse in the sea directly opposite Cahirciveen. Joanne Hayes was 'persuaded into believing' that she was the mother of the Cahirciveen baby, though Judge Lynch does not locate the source or describe the nature of the persuasion. The conclusion is invited that she persuaded herself and that it was her own guilty conscience which drove her to shout aloud that she was 'insane' and a 'murderess' who had 'killed her baby with a knife'. She was by then, after seven hours of interrogation, 'convinced', wrote the judge, that the Cahirciveen baby was hers. He did not find that the police convinced her of this. The irresistible conclusion is invited that her own family convinced her in various statements which the police merely brought to her attention.

In support of this the judge pointed out that no one but Joanne Hayes knew where the baby had been buried. The family, he wrote, had refused to help her dispose of the corpse and had asked no questions when it disappeared. A conclusion is invited that in their self-imposed state of terror in the police station, with by now only hazy memories of a night of terror on the farm, and in terrified ignorance of the finale of that night, the family convinced and falsely convicted each other, and misled a naive police force. The judge wound up his report of events in the police station by saying that the family had misunderstood that they were free to leave the station at any time, and the police had not made this adequately clear to them. He found no great fault with this breakdown in communication. It's the kind of thing that happens, the report implies, when cups of tea are supplied by the police to people who do not understand that they are voluntarily at a tea party which is no tea party at all. The judge recorded that

> Detective-Sergeant O'Carroll said to her that her baby would haunt her for the rest of her life. Whether or not he said this is of no great importance. It was not a tea-party they were at. The Gardaí were investigating the death of a baby that (inter alia) had been stabbed 28 times and had had its neck broken.

The judge did find that the police were to be faulted somewhat after the non-tea-party ended, charges were preferred and Joanne Hayes's baby was found. They had then resorted to 'unlikely, far fetched and self contradictory theories about twins to justify themselves'. The judge was quite scalding about this, though he had presided over a tribunal which had seemingly considered these theories.

Things are never what they seem, he conveyed in the most disingenuous sentence of the report. It was the statements made by the family to the police, and 'the family's insistence throughout the tribunal of a birth of a baby outside in the field' that 'made one wonder from time to time were there twins'. The judge knew perfectly well, this sentence invites the assumption, that the police and the lawyers and the experts were talking through their hats.

He did find that the police had 'gilded the lily' when testifying under oath to the tribunal. His attitude to this is quite playful, suggesting that boys will be boys in court, and that he knows when to take a tall tale with a pinch of salt. The police, he wrote, have to appear regularly in court and 'there is a danger that the Oath may become for them largely a matter of form. This does not mean that such a person is likely to tell completely groundless lies on Oath.'

This gilding of the relatively perfect police lily happens, he wrote, because 'familiarity breeds contempt'. Judge Kevin Lynch does not express undue upset at the contempt which the police showed for the oath, and for him and for the law when they presented their bunch of lilies to him during the tribunal. The police had merely engaged in a little 'exaggeration over and above the true position'. They had 'elevated wishful thinking to the status of hard fact'. The report does not ponder the awesome possibility flowing from such police attitudes: that if the Cahirciveen baby had been, perchance, blood-group O, such wishful thinking and gilding of the lily might have resulted in the imprisonment, upon conviction of murder, of Joanne Hayes and her family. The report has in fact laid grounds for fear – fear of the law itself, and of the courts, and of the police, because all that stands between the innocent and the opinion that the police are 'unlikely to tell completely groundless lies' is chance. Should chance dictate otherwise, people could end up in jail.

Having failed to satisfactorily solve the riddle of the 'additions' to the Hayes's confessions, the judge turned his attention from the million-pound central question of the tribunal to the secondary question that had clearly absorbed him – What happened on the farm that night? He confirmed at the outset that he was only surmising.

> This Chapter contains fewer references than most of the other Chapters in this Report, to the Transcripts of the Evidence given at the hearings of the Inquiry. The reason is that most of the facts found in this Chapter are so found by inference from other facts found in this Report, or by inference from evidence not directly supporting such facts, but indirectly doing so to the satisfaction of the Tribunal.

He distanced himself retrospectively from the completely contradictory evidence given by Bridie Fuller in the hospital – 'She is a suggestible witness and therefore her evidence must be approached by the tribunal with caution' – and found that in one respect she had been accurate. Bridie Fuller had cut the cord in the bedroom. Michael Hayes, he repeated, had grasped the explanation of the solemnity of the oath 'and immediately thereafter admitted' to witnessing birth in the bedroom. The judge then drew heavily on statements made in the police station to depict the scene.

> Joanne Hayes' mother, Mrs Mary Hayes, was very annoyed with Joanne Hayes and expressed her annoyance at the prospect of having to rear another child for Jeremiah Locke, especially when the child did not appear to be strong. Bridie Fuller and Kathleen Hayes also showed their displeasure to Joanne Hayes at her having another baby by Jeremiah Locke. Bridie Fuller left the room and went either to her own bedroom or to the kitchen.
>
> Joanne Hayes got into a panic and as the baby cried again she put her hands around its neck and stopped it crying by choking it and the baby did not breathe again. At some stage during the course of these events, Joanne Hayes used the bath brush from the bathroom to hit the baby to make sure that it was dead. None of the family tried to stop Joanne Hayes from either choking or hitting the baby.
>
> The whole family now got into a panic. Bridie Fuller had already left the room before the baby died. Ned Hayes was still sleeping below in the cottage and it was

decided that he should be sent for, as the eldest son and a person of considerable intelligence and imagination.

Nowhere in this carefully phrased scenario does the judge find that a criminal act has been committed by Joanne Hayes or her family. Given his reputation for accuracy and precision, it is regrettable that he couched his findings in language which could be, and was, widely misread by the legally untutored, who, he must have known, were hanging on his every word. The media, for example, interpreted the judge as saying that Joanne Hayes 'killed' her baby. He said no such thing. He is careful to avoid saying that she stopped her baby from breathing by choking it. In directly stating, however, that she 'stopped the crying by choking', Judge Lynch ran the serious risk of inviting the public to ask who the judge and Joanne Hayes were trying to kid. The popular understanding is that one chokes in order to stop breath, not cries, issuing from the throat. Joanne Hayes 'used the bathbrush' to hit the baby and 'make sure that it was dead'. One cannot, of course, kill a dead baby and again the judge accuses her of no crime, but the language unfortunately evokes in the unskilled mind an impression of a woman trying to make sure that a premeditated job – the killing of her child – was properly done. If the judge believed that a woman had gone sufficiently crazy to attack a dead child, he should perhaps have said so. The judge does not suggest that the family committed any crime, nor that they tried to assist Joanne Hayes in the commission of one. 'None of her family tried to assist Joanne Hayes in either choking or hitting the baby' would perhaps have given a clearer impression than the phrase he used: 'None of her family tried to stop' her. Were the family motivated by indifference or transfixed by horror? The judge does not say. The public is left to make up its own mind. The judge does offer some guidance to the public mind in striking an attitude to what would usually, on the evidence, be treated as the accidental death of a baby. Donning a moral cloak, the colours of which bear a striking resemblance to those of Catholic theology, Judge Kevin Lynch in this report depicts a family of such moral indifference and corruption that the wrath of God, transcending legal restraints, is called down upon them. The report implies that the source of this corruption is womanhood itself – no man was found to blame for the death of the Kerry babies, but the report infers that women can be saved from themselves. Women can be saved and elevated. The report suggests a distinction should be made between one kind of female and another. Women are saved and elevated to the status of ladies if they become mothers within marriage. Married mothers command respect, the unmarried mother and those women who associate with her activities are not ladies. Joanne Hayes and the women in her family, Mary Locke, wife of Jeremiah Locke, and Mary Moloney, wife of Liam Moloney the Abbeydorney policeman, are examples of the female sex about whom the judge asked the question during the tribunal, 'What kind of ladies are we dealing with here?' He found that Mary Moloney was 'the second most wronged woman' in the entire matter, the first being Mary Locke. Mary Locke had seen her husband enticed away from herself and her 'lawful' child, and Mary Moloney had miscarried her lawful child after receiving obscene phone calls which purported to defend Joanne Hayes. There was no third or fourth or fifth wronged woman. Joanne Hayes and her mother and sister were not, by implication, wronged ladies and Joanne got, by further implication, her just desert for her sexual activities outside of marriage – an illegitimate and bastard child called Yvonne, and the corpse of another illegitimate child.

Joanne Hayes was depicted by Judge Kevin Lynch as a sexually evil Eve, mesmerising a helpless Adam in the vale of Tralee. She 'had her eye on him. Joanne Hayes knew perfectly well of the marriage of Jeremiah Locke, yet a little over a year later Joanne Hayes had sexual intercourse with Jeremiah Locke'. Judge Lynch expressed regret that police laziness in tracing

Tom Flynn, the man who wrote his name on a mattress sold to the Hayes family in 1965, on which Joanne Hayes then slept, should have led to that man's character being tainted by association with her. A depraved public, the judge further implied, preferred adultery to marital fidelity. 'Why no flowers for Mrs Locke?' he asked, 'Why no cards or Mass cards? Why no public assemblies to support her in her embarrassment and agony? Is it because she married Jeremiah Locke and thus got in the way of the foolish hopes and ambitions of Joanne Hayes?'

The judge mistook as depravity the sensitivity of the public and media, who tactfully chose to accord Mary Locke the privacy to deal with her undoubted world of grief. The media fell for the moral blackmail of his virtual insistence that the public should now conduct an inquiry of their own into the feelings of Mary Locke. The reply which journalists brought back from her was a rebuke to a man who did not understand why Joanne Hayes's ordeal before him should have evoked such sympathy. 'Joanne Hayes was harshly treated,' said Mary Locke.

Given this attitude, the cold manner in which the judge treated the night in the farmhouse should have come as no surprise, but it did surprise and deeply wound those who entertained even the slightest hopes of sensitivity to the female condition.

While acknowledging that the birth was premature, the report takes no account of the implications of this – that whatever happened happened unexpectedly in the middle of the night, in an isolated house with no telephone, to women who could not drive a car, two of whom were elderly and in bad health, the third of whom was in the throes of labour, the fourth of whom had no experience of childbirth whatever. The report does not even acknowledge the pain, grief and silence which the pregnancy caused them long before the birth.

It is an undisputed fact that the first time any member of the family broke silence about the troubled pregnancy was when Kathleen Hayes went to her cousin's house in a desperate search for solace. Twenty-four hours later the birth was upon them. The cold and sparse scenario etched by Judge Kevin Lynch does not explore the dilemma of the Hayes women, or attempt to engage sympathy on their behalf, though an imaginative exploration would surely have done so. Had the judge been trying Joanne Hayes in court on a charge of infanticide, he would surely have been bound by the law he serves to show more compassion and mercy than he did when dealing with an accidental death, in his report. The law of this land reduces the charge of murder in such circumstances to infanticide, in recognition of the fact that childbirth and the rearing of an infant for the first year of its life are so stressful that a mother cannot be held fully accountable for her actions.

Wherever her baby was born, the body of Joanne Hayes burst open to allow it passage into the world. The gynaecologist testified that the flesh of her perineum tore apart. Dr Aidan Daly acknowledged that her blood poured forth in haemorrhage. Nowhere in a comment-studded report does the judge acknowledge the effects of such a birth on a woman's mind. Childbirth is no tea party.

This particular childbirth must have been pitifully hamfisted – the frail and elderly recluse Bridie Fuller cut the cord a wild fourteen inches from the infant's navel. The judge does not deal with the fact that there is absolutely no forensic evidence to show that she tied the cord after cutting it, or the consequences of failure to tie that cord. If the baby lived for half an hour with an untied cord, it should have spouted its life blood through the opened arteries of that cord and bled to death. Joanne Hayes's baby did not die of blood loss. No trace of blood spurts was found in her bedroom. The cord, speculated the state pathologist, was severed after death. This suggests that the baby died almost at once, after birth, in a scene of bedlam. Did Joanne Hayes, her body split open, try to stop the child crying while it was still bound to her by the umbilical cord? We will never know. The family insists that the baby was born in the field; the judge insists that the baby was born in the bedroom, and he declined to imagine the scene. He says that the bath-brush was used to strike an already dead child but makes no guess about the implications of this – that the baby died in seconds, since it takes only seconds for an infant that cannot breathe to pass from life to death (there was not sufficient time after birth for the child's lungs to inflate, the state pathologist found), that the family had no time to react, that they looked paralysed upon the scene and were even uncomprehending of the fact that the baby was dead, that Joanne Hayes, in a crazed state and bleeding, went to the bathroom and returned with a bathbrush with which she then attacked her baby, that the family thought they were then witnessing a deliberate killing and that they subsequently tried to protect her by not telling the full story of what they thought they had witnessed. One can conjure up any number of scenarios, all of them involving fear and distress and elderly and young panic-stricken women. Another alternative scenario is one of cold and deliberate inac-tivity. It is impossible, unless one casts a cold and distasteful eye upon womanhood, to share the judge's opinion (and it is no more than an opinion) that Mary Hayes was 'especially annoyed when the child did not appear to be strong'. The infer-ence is that she actually welcomed its death, not just because it was illegitimate, but because it was a sickly little bastard as well. The judge does not ask why children are categorised as illegitimate or wonder if that stigma would 'persuade' people that such babies are unwelcome in Ireland. This family lied in the belief that a story of death in the field would render them 'not all that blameworthy', the judge found.

The report throws down a ferocious gauntlet – will compas-sion be grudgingly extended only if a woman has proved that she truly suffered, in the dark, in the cold, in the open air, as Anne Lovett suffered and died, and as Joanne Hayes claims she suffered and survived, but will that compassion be withheld if a woman has the effrontery to give birth in bed, though the reason for secret birth (in this case unexpected birth) is exactly the same – troubled and unwanted pregnancy. A question haunts the report – by whom are children unwanted. Is the Hayes family to be isolated and carry blame entirely and is it seriously suggested that Irish society is standing proudly by waiting for the child, any child, no matter the circumstances of its parentage. Such an attitude suggests that Irishwomen are motivated by nothing other than individual, selfish, wilful indifference to abandon their newborn in railway stations, in telephone kiosks and before the altars of their God. That Kerry women in particular do not kill their babies before abandoning them is a matter of sheer chance: the judge points out that there are two illegitimate births in Kerry every week and asks, in this context, 'what is so unbelievably extraordinary about two women attempting to do away with their babies in the same week?' The phrase bears repetition: 'attempting to do away with their babies'. The newborn do not die because their mothers are distraught and in social fear. The newborn die because their mothers 'do away with' them in the mode of Herod. Diabolical! Woman as anti-Christ! to borrow the exclamation marks with which this man's report is studded. There is an unfortunate and careless echo of diabolism in the judge's description of Joanne Hayes as a woman who 'dominated' her family and her lover. The tribunal had hard evidence, from a psychiatrist, of another woman who so dominated her family that she persuaded them that she had had sexual intercourse with the devil. The judge settles for suggesting that Joanne Hayes was not in the diabolical but the French tradition: he refers to her 'affaire' with Jeremiah Locke. A vision is conjured up of sexually repressed Irish males in the Fifties when they wondered what the hell Brigitte Bardot was up to that the censorship board would not allow them to watch her in the movie *And God Created Woman*.

This report's attitude to sexual relations between men and women is such, if it fairly represents the male view of women.

Will this report be enough to drive Irishwomen and their children off the cliffs of Slea Head in suicidal despair? The apparent contrast between the restrained language which the judge employed in assessing the truthfulness of police witnesses who gilded the lily, and the moral virulence of his criticism of the Hayes family, barefaced liars who feared to tell him what he thought was the full truth, is less astonishing when placed in the context of the last few years. In 1983 Bishop Joseph Cassidy declared that the most dangerous place in the world is in a woman's womb. It is in the womb that the actions and consequences of male sexual behaviour are made flesh. By limiting the male role to taking 'what' is available and imposing on women total responsibility for the babies that might result, a conclusion may be drawn that the male buck stops at the entrance to the womb. After that, woman is to blame.

Her part is to sit, as Joanne Hayes and Kathleen Hayes and Mary Hayes must now sit, in the farmhouse, while a tour bus pulls up on the road outside and the guide tells the story of the Kerry babies.

Their grief might be eased if people start asking why, not what. Their isolation might be eased if Irish society takes responsibility for surrounding certain pregnancies with odium. Their pain might be shared if Irishwomen speak aloud the anguished truth of their condition. This writer is grateful that this book affords the opportunity to record publicly and permanently her love, sympathy and respect for the Hayes family, and her admiration for the people of Abbeydorney who reached out and stood by their neighbours.